Estate Planning
When You Have Pets

Estate Planning
When You Have Pets

Kelli E. Brown, J.D., LL.M.

Copyright 2019 Kelli E. Brown
Publisher:
October Day Publishing, LLC
Louisville, Kentucky 40059

Cover Design : Created from the original art of Maddie Hawkins
Designed by VIA Studios, Louisville, Kentucky

Edited by Anne Cole, New York

Editions ISBN
Soft Cover
PDF

Brown, Kelli
        Estate Planning When You Have Pets
        Includes bibliographical references, index and appendices

ISBN 13: 978-0-9983009-3-1

LCCN: 2019909101

October Day Publishing, LLC, Louisville, Kentucky

Bulk orders:

Quantity discounts are available on bulk purchases of this book for educational and training purposes. Discounts are also available to schools, organizations, libraries, community centers, corporations, and others. To learn more, contact us at octoberdaypublishing@gmail.com or October Day Publishing, LLC, Louisville, Kentucky.

How to contact the author:

Kelli E. Brown is a practicing attorney in Kentucky. She focuses her practice in the areas of estate planning, probate, estate litigation, and estate administration. She is a frequent speaker on all aspects of estate planning and probate. To contact Ms. Brown for an interview, speaking engagement, or personal appearance, please visit her website, www.estateplanningbooks.com, or e-mail her at kellibrownattorney@gmail.com.

Readers of this book are encouraged to contact the author with constructive comments and ideas for future editions.

WARNING AND DISCLAIMER

Even though I practice law for a living, this book is not intended to provide you with legal advice; rather, it is informational in nature, written by an attorney who has been there and done that in the area of estate planning for many years. Your issues are specific to you, and for legal advice, you should retain your own attorney in the state in which you live and consult him or her about your situation.

If you have read the above, I am sure that you already know that I am not your attorney; however, my law firm and my malpractice carrier require me to tell you this again, here, in writing, in this book. So, consider that done. If you happen to live in Kentucky, please feel free to research me and other qualified attorneys who practice estate planning and probate in your area who may be able to assist you with your legal needs.

It's important to me that you understand that even though the laws of your state may or may not specifically provide for estate planning for your pet, there are still estate planning techniques that may be employed to benefit your pets, including the many options mentioned in this book.

Also, please know that this is not a book with "do-it-yourself" forms. It's not because I don't like you, I do (thanks for buying my book), it's because I think that forms are for a one-size-fits-all situation, and in my opinion estate planning is not that.

Lastly, please understand that there is a whole big, wide world of federal and state tax issues that could apply upon your death, even if you leave assets to a pet. I do not address those tax issues in this book predominantly because if you are leaving assets to a pet, like me, I assume you do not care about the tax consequences of doing so. Yet, consulting a qualified estate planning attorney about your situation should mean that any and all tax consequences from your death would be addressed by *that* competent counsel. Therefore, I will leave the tax stuff to him or her and you and I can talk about the interesting stuff.

ACKNOWLEDGMENTS

I greatly appreciate the many people who have positively influenced my life. There are many.

Thank you to the lawyers that trained me, Charles E. English and Wade T. Markham, II. Thank you to my clients. They make practicing law meaningful. It is my honor to be trusted to perform your work.

I could not practice law without the help of qualified assistants, paralegals, and attorneys. Over the years, I have been privileged to work with a spectacular group. Special thanks to Valerie Crowell for all that you do.

Thank you to my draft "readers" of this book, especially Ellen Brown-Geers and Deborah Campbell. Not only did you read my first draft, you made suggestions, helped me to focus on important topics, and provided the enthusiasm that I needed. My most sincere thanks.

Any success in my life would not have come without the support and efforts of my family, including my parents, David and Linda Brown; the World's Best Husband, Walter; and especially the sunshine and happiness of my life, my children, Henry and Madeline, and Holly (fur child).

This book is dedicated to all the pets who have touched my life especially --
Nicky, Sophie, Claire, Lieutenant, Frankie, Dickel, Dallas, George, Mozzie,
Maebe, and my sweet Holly.

Holly

CONTENTS

INTRODUCTION

My husband and I decided early on that we had our hands full with our responsibilities to our human children and therefore a pet did not fit into our lives. We tried to make that as clear as we could to our children from the start. When our oldest child was twelve, he and his sister (then eight) prepared a PowerPoint presentation entitled "Why We Need a Pet." They argued that a pet would teach responsibility ("We will feed it!"); it would provide exercise ("We will walk it!"); and, most persuasively, they would learn about loss, which would prepare them for the inevitable loss of a family member (Geez…).

My husband and I applauded the effort, but we were initially a firm "no." However, the PowerPoint did make an impression on us, as it raised some interesting issues. It may not be enough for children to pet-sit for others, we thought, and to only enjoy the company of a neighbor's pet. We pondered whether perhaps our children might actually need to experience the benefits and detriments of having a pet in *our* home.

Although allergies in the family ruled out most cats and dogs, we opened the door to the possibility of finding the *right* pet for us. There was a fish incident that we don't talk about (no, we did *not* know that tap water would be harmful) … "water friends" were ruled out. We ultimately decided that perhaps a dog might work for us, and we gave it some real thought.

One day in December 2016, almost Christmas, my daughter and I had a chance encounter with a stranger carrying an adorable puppy. Since my daughter threw herself at the pup, I had time to engage in small talk with this very patient and kind fur mom. The woman shared that her pup did not shed, would not grow very big, and was easy to potty train. Music to my ears. We looked online, we called, we researched, and almost a year later, Holly, a nine-week old mini-poodle ball of fur came to be part of our family.

I would like to tell you that my kids take care of Holly and I do nothing. Not so. But the truth is, she is an absolute joy. A sweet and fun, kiss-your-face, want-to-sleep-next-to-you, please-let-me-sit-next-to-you, let's-go-to-the-park, little tail-wagger of happiness. She is part of the family and the only one on the planet who thinks that I rule the universe. Suddenly, I am *that* pet person who talks baby-talk to the dog and kisses her on her face, and I just cannot believe that I am not allowed to take her with me every single place I go, including grocery shopping and to work.

After Holly came into my life, I knew that my own estate planning needed to be updated to include her. And then I realized that pets in estate planning would be a fun topic to write a book about. This new book would be a light topic for "pet parents" who, like me, are of the opinion that including your pets in your estate planning is important.

I did, however, worry a little about how a pet estate planning book would be received by my clients and colleagues. For some people a pet is just a pet, and to them, recognizing a pet in your estate planning documents might seem outlandish. Then I decided that while I do know that my dog is not my actual offspring, she is part of my family. We adopted her. We love her. We are responsible for her care, including her food, shelter, and well-being. She loves us and brings joy, and it is my responsibility to say what should happen to her if my family cannot take care of her. I turned to my friends and many of my longtime clients to inquire about this topic and found much enthusiasm. Thus, here we are.

This book has been fun to write. It is designed to explore the details of what you need to know to include your pets in your estate planning including estate planning basics, the mechanics of the actual documents, and techniques that I use for myself and my actual clients to help them get the plan that they want. It also suggests ways to choose the right people to help you and provides checklists to get you to the point where you're ready to address your estate planning needs regarding your pet or pets.

I hope that if you are reading this book, and it's appropriate to your situation, you will benefit from the information and enjoy it. If this book has helped you, and if you are willing, please drop me a line or go to my Facebook or Instagram and share with me a picture of your fur baby.

Part One

Pet Estate Planning - Oh Yes You Can!

CHAPTER 1

Providing For Your Pets: An Overview

When I was a relatively new lawyer, I handled probate for the estate of an elderly widowed gentleman who had recently passed. I had not met him before he died and I did not prepare his estate planning documents. The adult children (all sons) came in from out of state with their wives and we met at my office. They brought with them the elderly man's beloved dog, a little poodle type who was scared to death and shaking. The wives wanted to know immediately if the dog could be "put down" before they loaded up the old man's possessions and headed home back to their lives. I even remember the dog's name; for our purposes, let's call her "Susie." My staff and I were horrified. Poor Susie! It was evident to us that these wives wanted to ransack the deceased man's valuables and certainly did not consider little Susie's life to be important.

My assistant was a pet advocate and we spoke to the family about releasing Susie to a local shelter. Although the family agreed they would indeed turn Susie over to a shelter instead of having her "put down," I have zero proof that this actually occurred. I have never, ever forgotten this. My hope is that Susie was indeed adopted and lived the rest of her life with a person or family that loved her and that she loved.

Had I met with the man before he passed away, I might have asked him whether he wanted to make provisions for his Susie. Maybe I would've inquired about who should take her and whether any funds be set aside for her. Perhaps he would have declined, thinking that he would outlive Susie, or he may have thought it was silly to plan for a pet. We will never know.

Here's what we do know, however: Had the man given some thought to little Susie and how her life would be different when he passed, my staff and I wouldn't have had to convince the adult children to save Susie's life.

Including your pets in estate planning is a real thing and it *is* important. Consider, there are an estimated 95.6 million cats and 83.3 million dogs in American households. There are also 20.6 million birds, 8.3 million horses, 145 million freshwater fish, 13.6 million saltwater fish, 11.6 million reptiles, and 18.1 million other small animals. Wow. Americans have a lot of pets and it follows that if something happens to a pet owner, the pet will have to go someplace else and still need care. For some of my clients and for myself, it's essential to plan for what happens to our pets if something happens to us.

The above real-life example shows that without advanced estate planning the situation for your pet can be perilous. There are many options out there for pet owners and planning. This chapter explores the basics of why pet estate planning is important.

No Need to Be Embarrassed

While estate planning strikes many people as complex, and it can be in some circumstances, the essentials are pretty simple with the right help. Basically, estate planning means talking to a lawyer about drafting legal documents that say what will happen in the event of your incapacity or death. Things like who gets your stuff and money, when they get it, and who is in charge if for some reason you cannot act for yourself or if you die.

Do not be embarrassed to address issues related to your pet or pets as part of your estate planning. For well over a decade, the estate planning questionnaire that I give to clients to complete before they meet with me specifically inquires whether the client wants to provide for a pet in estate planning.

Many states have specific laws in place for estate planning for pets; even if yours does not, your estate planning documents can make arrangements for your pets. Many options are available to you.

Protecting Your Fur Baby

Some people automatically think that they will outlive their pets, but this may not be the case. If you are a pet parent and incapacity or death comes when it's unexpected, your poor pet may be left out in the cold. Including your pet in your estate planning can make sure he/she is protected and put your mind at ease. It does so by addressing the following:

- Who will take care of my pet if I suddenly cannot?
- What will happen to my pet if I die?
- Who will be in charge of making sure my pet goes to the right person or place?
- Who will pay the pet costs if I die or become incapacitated?

If done right, estate planning can provide the answer for all of those questions.

If You Don't Protect Your Fur Baby

When a person dies or becomes incapacitated and there isn't any estate planning in place, pets are generally treated as personal property. This is because you *own* your pets in the same way that you own your furnishings and dishes.

In most cases, if something happens to the pet's family, then either the pets go to a family member who volunteers to take them or to the local shelter. One need only walk the aisles at a pet store that houses pet adoptions to learn that a pet is adoptable because the "owner passed away" or "owner went into nursing home." It happens all the time.

Without advanced estate planning the situation for your pet can be hazardous. Here are some common situations:

A pet will be "put down." I cannot imagine why placing an unwanted pet with an entity that does adoptions would not be the *first* course of action and death the last. A properly drafted directive in your Last Will and Testament together with a small sum of money can likely prevent a death sentence for your pet.

A pet will be placed with a local no-kill organization. There are organizations in many communities that were formed to help animals in need. Kind people dedicate their time to making sure that animals are given the opportunity to be cared for. If you aren't aware of anyone who could take your pet, having he/she placed with one of these groups could mean re-adoption and a happy life.

A pet will be given to the local (kill) shelter. Some towns only have kill shelters. If your pet is young and cute, then this is not necessarily the worst option because he or she is likely to get adopted. However, if your pet is older and/or has medical issues, he or she could be at risk of not being adopted and ultimately put down. There are many options in your estate planning documents which could prevent this—we will get into them in Chapter 4.

A pet will be released into the neighborhood. I am not sure what kind of person does this, but we all know it happens. There are just so many bad possibilities when this occurs. It is frustrating that anyone would do this.

A pet will be given to a random family member. This could be great for the pet or not so great. Most of us can make a list of family and friends entitled "these people would be wonderful pet parents" and another list called "no way should these people be pet parents." If you don't plan for your pet, it's possible he/she could end up with someone on the latter list.

I am obsessed with animal rescue shows and news stories and videos about pet rescues; if you also watch them, you know that there are some people who live in deplorable conditions with pets. There are also plenty of individuals or families who would provide a safe and loving environment for a pet. The issue is that if you do not address to whom your pet goes in your estate planning, then decisions regarding their fate will be made by someone other than you.

Come Prepared

In a perfect estate planning world, the process for an estate plan that includes your pets would go like this:

Seek out information. Reading this book means that you can figure out what you want regarding your pets before you meet with an attorney, that you understand how the process works, and have a plan in mind. There is a world of possibilities out there from the simple to the complex. Being informed is the key to having a positive experience with estate planning, which translates into your wishes being reflected for all of your loved ones, including your furry ones.

Find the right lawyer for you. Not all lawyers are created equal and not every attorney is the one for you. This is especially true when it comes to estate planning. There is no shame in realizing that the lawyer you are meeting with is not the one for you. I suggest that you find one of the age, gender, and experience that makes you feel comfortable; someone who will be fair with the fee, and who is smart and attentive. I provide more guidance about these important issues in Chapter 8.

Come prepared. Go into a meeting with an attorney with some idea of what you want so you can avoid overlooking any details. For example, you may have thought of who will take your pets if you cannot have them (a "Pet Custodian"). There are other issues, though, such as whether you'd like to allocate money for the care of your pet; this is something to consider.

Finalize your Estate Plan. Once your estate planning documents are drafted and they reflect your wishes, you sign them and then keep the original documents in a safe location. Your important people (those named in your document who will act in the event of your incapacity or death) need to know where your documents are kept. Plan on re-visiting your estate planning with your attorney every three to five years or when there is some life-changing event that will impact the provisions in your documents.

A Member of the Family

Estate planning is a process you should want to complete. It takes care of your family in a very profound way by stating who should get your assets, who should be in charge, and how the assets will be distributed. If you consider your pet to be part of your family, then it's not surprising that you'd want him/her to be included in this undertaking.

When I thought of all of the love my little tail-wagging fur baby gives to our family, I happily included her in my estate plan.

CHAPTER 2

When You Need A Hand: Taking Care Of Fur Babies In The Event Of Your Incapacity

There could be a time in your life when you cannot act for yourself. Maybe you're sick, injured, or elderly; it happens. Or you can act for yourself but you're not around to take care of your affairs – you might go away on an extended trip. If this occurs, someone will need to step in -- someone who will help pay the bills, keep the lights on, and take care of the fur babies. There are documents that address this situation; however, most of the time people overlook how necessary it is to have them.

Many years ago, when I first became an attorney, an elderly lady with pets asked me to make provisions for them in her Last Will document. We did so and when she was signing the papers she inquired what would happen to her pets if she was alive but could not act for herself. As this was before I established my pet policies, I recall that I responded with a shrug and indicated that perhaps whoever was handling her money as her Power of Attorney would make good "pet" decisions. Right then and there she told me to re-draft her Power of Attorney document to specify that her funds should be used for the care and keeping of her pets. She was right to demand this and I did so.

Since then, pet provisions are common in all of the estate planning documents that I draft. Many times I include language that allows for pets to be maintained if pet parents are not able to act for themselves. This chapter will explain what documents you need to have on file in case you became incapacitated and the practical applications as applied to pets.

Power of Attorney Documents

Most states have laws that allow you to designate a person to handle your financial business via what is often referred to as a "Power of Attorney" document.

There is such confusion over this important legal tool—for many, it's unclear what it does or how to use it. Basically, a Power of Attorney designation gives someone the power to act for you. Although there are different kinds of Power of Attorney documents, the kind discussed in this book are the ones that control your financial life -- your money, your assets, your bill paying, and the use of your money to take care of your pets.

Consider for a moment how powerful it is to allow someone to act for you financially. Most of us would not just turn over our checking account to anyone. I would not. In fact, many of us were taught from an early age that our finances were private and not to be discussed. So you may be asking yourself, *why would I ever do this?* The answer is that if something happens to you and you cannot handle your financial world anymore, planning ahead and having a Power of Attorney can keep your finances safe and in order. Doing a Power of Attorney means the following:

1) You get to choose the best person to do the job.
2) You get to determine ahead of time the parameters of what he or she can do.

Having these decisions spelled out and structured as enforceable under your state laws is a very good thing to do. An absence of a Power of Attorney can create chaos: if something happens to you, no one is legally in charge and no one has access to your financial resources.

What Happens Without a Power of Attorney

Your state has laws in place that dictate what happens if you cannot act for yourself and you have no Power of Attorney. The laws vary from state to state; in my state, having someone take over for a person who is incapacitated means that the court becomes involved, the incapacitated person gets assigned an attorney, various medical professionals are hired to assess the person, there is an actual jury trial, and the judge appoints an individual to be in charge and then report to the court about his or her actions. Contrast that "process" with the one in which you planned ahead, completed a Power of Attorney, and designated the right person to act, establishing boundaries that are specific to his or her situation. The difference is that setting things up in advance allows you to designate the individual who should be in charge. This means that family members are not left guessing (or fighting!) about it. It also saves time and money from lawyers and court intervention.

What Are the Different Kinds of Power of Attorney Documents?

There are many different kinds of Powers of Attorney documents because there are many different situations where a person may need to give someone else the ability to act for him or her. Here are a few examples of different types of Power of Attorney documents and their uses:

- **Special/limited Power of Attorney:** This allows you to designate someone for a specific purpose or a limited use or time period. For example, if you are taking a trip of a lifetime to Europe and will be gone for a prolonged period of time, you can sign a special Power of Attorney allowing the person of your choice to act on your behalf while you're away.

- **General Power of Attorney.** This document is active as soon as you sign it, which means that the person whom you appoint (sometimes called an "attorney-in-fact" or "agent") can act immediately. These are the most common.
- **Springing Power of Attorney.** This type of Power of Attorney cannot be used unless there is some sort of triggering event, such as incapacity. Attorneys sometimes refer to them as springing Powers of Attorney because they do not "spring" into action unless a certain event (likely incapacity) occurs.

Pet Provisions in a Power of Attorney Document

11

A good estate plan for pet parents can and should include provisions for your pets in a Power of Attorney document that would take effect if you are living but for some reason cannot take care of them. Here are a few ideas that I sometimes employ:

Appoint a Pet Custodian. "Pet Custodian" is a term I use to refer to the person who would take care of your pet in the event of your incapacity. There are a variety of situations in which a Pet Custodian would be needed; here's one example:

> *Jane is a single person with an eight-year-old cat named Featherbell. Jane adores Featherbell but not everyone she knows feels the same way; it may be more accurate to say that Featherbell does not love anyone but Jane and a select group of people, including Jane's brother, Todd. Featherbell sheds and he requires a lot of attention. Sometimes he can be mean. Jane is concerned that if something happens to her, Featherbell would be hard to place or worse, go to a shelter that would perhaps put him down. The problem is that Todd is not good with finances and he lives paycheck to paycheck; she's not sure if he could afford to take good care of Featherbell. Jane's estate planning attorney drafts a Power of Attorney document stating that if she becomes incapacitated, her brother, Todd, will be Featherbell's Pet Custodian and her other brother, John, will handle Jane's money. The designation of the Pet Custodian includes language that allows Todd to take Featherbell to his home or to stay in Jane's home with Featherbell. It further states that John is required to give Todd (the Pet Custodian) money for Featherbell's needs including his vet bills, kitty litter, toys, and food.*

In the above example, those involved in Jane's life know her wishes because she wrote them down in a legal way with the help of a real attorney. Had language about a Pet Custodian been missing from Jane's document, John, who would likely have been appointed to be in charge of Jane's money and personal affairs, could have given Featherbell away, thinking that it would just be easier. But because Jane planned ahead, it means that in the event of her incapacity, her brothers will know that her pet is a priority and is to be taken care of. It also means that if necessary, the Pet Custodian can require the person in charge of the money to comply with the terms. Which in turn means that even if John thinks that taking care of Featherbell is a silly thing to do, he can't withhold money from Todd to be used for that purpose.

When a person becomes unable to handle his or her affairs, those in charge often just handle what they deem important, which is usually the money part – they keep the lights on, for instance, and make the mortgage payment. If the person you appoint to take care of things is great with money but would not give much thought to your fur baby, you have an issue that could (and should!) be addressed in your estate planning documents.

If you would like to name someone as Pet Custodian, it's a good idea to ask that person, as he or she needs to be willing to do the job, and then-- if they say yes--notify them about the documents in which they are named.

Of course, this person should be the right choice for the job. I have had this conversation with my designated Pet Custodian and I will admit, it feels strange because it means that my spouse and I would somehow not be able to act. Yet making sure our pet is cared for by the right person is important to us and therefore we have provided for this in our documents.

Allow the disbursement of funds for your pet. Sometimes we have people in our lives who are skeptical of spending money on the needs of a pet. You and I might agree that having a tumor removed from the ear of a beloved bunny is a good idea; however, the person we appoint to oversee our finances if we are incapacitated might think differently. My feeling is that it is *your* money and what is important to you rules the day.

Your Power of Attorney document can specifically allow for the distribution of your money for the needs of a pet. For example, a document could say something like:

> *"I hereby grant my Attorney-in-fact the ability to utilize my funds and assets via my designated Pet Custodian or other person for the purpose of the care, feeding, and maintenance of my pets including but not limited to my dog and bunny and any other pets I may own. Care, feeding and maintenance shall include but not be limited to food, pet supplies, pet toys, veterinary services, pet day care, grooming, and preventative care. It is my intent that in the event of my in-*

capacity, my pets be taken care of consistent with the care and treatment I provided to those pets when I had the ability and capacity to act."

It can be very specific. Remember, this is *you* saying what is important. Here's another scenario where a Pet Custodian was needed:

Dave is a fifty-something man who lives alone, with adult children living out of state. He has an energetic dog, Belle, who he adores. When Dave is out of the house all day, he sends Belle to doggy daycare, which costs twenty-five dollars a day. Belle loves it and Dave is happy that Belle is having fun and getting exercise. Dave is having a very serious surgery and his recovery means that he will be in an assisted living facility for at least two months. He is concerned that while he is recovering, his sister (who is the person he appointed to handle his money in his Power of Attorney document) would put Belle in a crate all day and check on her only once. Dave hires an attorney, designates a pet-loving neighbor as Belle's Pet Custodian and includes language that allows his money to be used for Belle. The document specifically requires that Belle continue going to doggie daycare, and further states that Dave's sister is required to give the Pet Custodian money for Belle's other needs including vet bills and food. Dave speaks with his sister and the Pet Custodian about the Power of Attorney document and his wishes while he is recovering. Although Dave's sister thinks this is not a good use of his money, he knows what Dave's wishes are and promises to be respectful.

In the above example, Dave's important people know his priorities. Even though his sister may not agree that doggie daycare is a good use of his funds, it's Dave's direction that matters.

Common Questions About Powers of Attorney

What is a "Durable" Power of Attorney?

A power of attorney that is "durable" is one that remains in place even though the person giving the power becomes incapacitated. The vast majority of powers of attorney that are signed for estate planning are "durable" since planning for incapacity is one of the primary reasons to have this document in the first place.

Choosing the Right Type of Power of Attorney Document for You

Many people choose to have a "general" Power of Attorney (one that is active when you sign it) that is also durable (one that will continue to be valid even if you become incapacitated). However, some people feel strongly that a Power of Attorney document should not become active unless he or she becomes incapacitated (a "springing" Power of Attorney).

Many times when I am including pet provisions in a Power of Attorney document, I recommend a general Power of Attorney. This is because I want the person appointed to have the ability to act immediately should something occur. What if, for example, my contingency to activate the Power of Attorney is that my doctor has to agree that incapacity has occurred but when I had a traumatic medical event, my doctor was out of town for three weeks? Suddenly, the person named under the document could be scrambling around trying to find a replacement doctor. However, while a general Power of Attorney erases any contingencies, it's nonetheless still not for everyone. These documents are powerful; they actually give someone who is not you the power to *be* you for money purposes. That's a lot of power.

A springing Power of Attorney can provide an extra layer of protection of your finances because it can require that certain people (like a doctor) say that you cannot act for yourself. For instance, if your Power of Attorney was stolen by someone who then tried to use it at your bank, your local teller might see that the document requires a certificate from your physician to be "active" and know that something isn't right. Such contingencies can provide peace of mind. Another situation where a springing Power of Attorney can be helpful is if someone who is sick or elderly is concerned that family members would be too quick to "take over" when he or she is not ready for that.

The point is for you to designate the right person to be able to make good financial decisions for you if you cannot make those decisions for yourself in a document that comports with the specifics of your situation.

Whether the ability to act is now or contingent upon your incapacity, know that the Power of Attorney document can include language that ensures your funds can be used for food, shelter, and care of your fur babies.

When Does a Power of Attorney End?

A Power of Attorney can end by several means, including the following:

Revocation by Death: A Power of Attorney document ends at your death. Several times a year, I get a phone call from an adult child who tells me that his or her parent died and he or she has "the Power of Attorney" for that parent. I tell him/her that Powers of Attorney are only for the living. Once someone passes away, the Power of Attorney dies with that person. The individual in charge becomes a personal representative such as an Executor or an Administrator.

Revocation by Writing: There are many ways to do this, however, the best way is often to sign a written document that revokes the Power of Attorney. The next step would be to notify the person who had the ability to act for you under the document that his or her power is void. Then provide the written revocation to the people and entities that were given copies of the Power of Attorney document. Of course, it is important to have your attorney draft an updated Power of Attorney.

Revocation by Provisions in the Power of Attorney Document: Sometimes the language in a Power of Attorney document will state that the document is valid for a certain period of time or upon the happening of a certain event. For example, a Power of Attorney to sell a certain parcel of real estate may say that the document will be in effect until after the real estate closing or until a certain date, such as December 31st of the year in which the sale will take place.

Revocation by the Court: Another way that a Power of Attorney can be revoked is by and through a court order. In some states, if the person who signed the Power of Attorney is declared incompetent by the court and a guardianship is instituted, the Power of Attorney is revoked (and overridden). In addition, if a Power of Attorney is obtained through fraud or other unscrupulous means, then a court may order that the document be terminated.

Does a Power of Attorney control my health care decisions too?

It depends on your state. Many times, a state will have a document that is called a "living will" or a "health care directive," separate from a Power of Attorney, that allows you to make decisions concerning your health. In my opinion, your money decisions and your health decisions should not be contained in the same document. Your bank, for instance, does not need to know whether you want to be kept on life support.

Checklist for Pet Planning In The Event of Your Incapacity

- Determine whether you would like to appoint a Pet Custodian
- Determine what the duties and obligations would be:
  - Location (pet stays in the home or goes to a specific place)
  - Health care
  - Food
  - Day care
- Decide on an alternate Pet Custodian (if the one you appoint cannot act)
- Have a conversation with the Pet Custodian about the specifics and his or her willingness to act
- If your Pet Custodian is not the same person as the person who will be your Attorney-in-fact (the person you designate under your Power of Attorney document to handle your finances), make sure that your Attorney-in-fact is aware of the Pet Custodian appointment.
- Locate an estate planning attorney who will draft the documents with the above in mind

CHAPTER 3

Estate Planning When You Have Pets: The Basics

I t drives me bonkers when someone dies without a Last Will and Testament. Even though this means more work (and therefore more money) for me and other estate planning attorneys, it usually makes things difficult and chaotic for the family of the person who died.

In my opinion, an estate plan is a gift to those we leave behind. I know this to be true because I bear witness to what happens inside families when someone dies *without* estate planning documents. In this situation, family members tend to become frustrated when I explain that state law will dictate everything that happens, including who gets what, when they get it, and who may apply to be in charge. They argue that even though their loved one did not have a Will, they know what he or she wanted. That may be true (or not true) depending upon the circumstances, but it is not relevant to how the estate is handled. The law is what it is, so to speak, so after death I cannot change how things unfold. This has the potential to cause problems and hard feelings that did not have to occur had the deceased person taken the time to do a Will.

With regard to your pets, not having an estate plan in place can be particularly problematic. Pets are considered your "property." You own them. Thus, power over a deceased person's pets is determined either by estate planning documents or by the law of the state in which the deceased person lived if there are no estate planning documents.

This chapter explains the basics of estate planning. Understanding the basics means that you can look at your situation and apply what you learn for the purpose of making good decisions for your family, including your fur babies.

Last Will and Testament Fundamentals

In this section we'll cover the basic documents associated with estate planning in contemplation of death. A Last Will and Testament is usually the centerpiece of any plan for many reasons, not the least of which is that it's a public declaration of someone's final desires at the time of death. It's literally a person's last written words about his or her wishes.

A Last Will and Testament is a declaration meant to apply after death that determines who gets what and when they get it, who is in charge, and how they are in charge. The concept is simple—at some point, our lives will be over, and the people we leave behind will have to attend to the legal issues of our lives. The Last Will and Testament document is the road map for how to do this. Here is some basic information about Wills:

Wills are revocable: During your lifetime (and while you have the mental capacity to do so and have not contracted yourself otherwise), your Last Will and Testament can be revoked, changed, or amended.

Standards for a valid Will: A Last Will and Testament is a document of death only. Most states require that to be valid, a Will must meet the following criteria:

- It must be a written document signed by the person making it.
- The person making it must be competent.
- The person making it must be age eighteen or older.
- The person making it must be under no undue influence or duress.
- It must be signed in the presence of witnesses (many states say two).
- Some states require that a notary be present. While it may not be required, having a notary public sign the document can make it easier for probate.

Content of a Will: Generally, the content of a Last Will document is broken up into three categories:

- who gets the asset under a Last Will;

- who is in charge of a Last Will and Testament; and
- the rules under which the person in charge (your Executor) can act.

What Is Probate?

Probate? Cue the piercing horror film scream. Most people shudder upon hearing the word, but probate has a reputation that it does not deserve. The truth is that sometimes probate is necessary.

Probate is the procedure in which a will is proven to be valid. In many states, probate requires that assets of a deceased person be given to the correct person via a court-ordered process. It permits the person in charge to legally wrap up the legal affairs of a person's life and then give his/her assets to each respective person designated in the Will. If the deceased person did not have a Will, there is a process in which the assets are given to family members in a certain order (like spouse and children).

When I have assets going through probate I have an awesome boss (i.e. the judge) who makes sure that things run on time and, importantly, that the Will of the dead person is respected. This is important because most pets do not have title. Title means what name the "asset" (in this case, your pet) is in and whether or not you have designated a co-owner or a beneficiary separate from the Will. Thus, with pets, your Will can control who takes them and who gets the provisions for their care.

Assets that Pass under a Last Will and Testament

Depending upon the laws in your state, only certain assets may be subject to your Last Will and Testament. In many states, *how* you title an asset may mean that the asset is or is not subject to your Last Will and Testament. This is very important. Consider when you go to your bank and open a checking account that you have many options for title/ownership, including:

- your own name alone;
- owned jointly with another person; or
- owned by you but there is a "pay on death" or "transfer on death" beneficiary.

So many options! And importantly, the title that you choose matters very much if you should die. For example, many times, if you have an asset that is titled "jointly to the survivor" and the "survivor" is alive when you die, then that survivor gets the asset by just submitting proof of your death, such as a death certificate. That asset will pass to that person without going to probate and will therefore not be subject to your Last Will and Testament. Similarly, a "pay on death" designation or a beneficiary designation (as with life insurance or retirement) works the same way. I find that a great deal of people (even sometimes lawyers) do not seem to know this information and are surprised to find it out.

Here's an example of how title to an asset dictates whether it will or will not be subject to a Will:

> *Joe dies with $100,000 in a savings account and with few other assets. During his life, Joe's banker suggested that to avoid probate, Joe name one of his children as a "pay on death" beneficiary. Joe completed the bank documents and named Allie, his oldest child, as the "pay on death" beneficiary. Joe's Last Will and Testament says that he leaves his beloved elderly dog to his friend, Tim, as the Pet Custodian. It also leaves 10% of assets to his dog with Tim in charge of the money. When Joe dies, Tim gets the dog, but Allie goes to the bank and the bank indicates that she (and only she) gets the $100,000. Allie can share but that money legally belongs to her and she decides not to do so. Since there are not any assets passing through Joe's Will, there is nothing for Joe's dog. Tim will need to figure out if he can keep Joe's dog given all of the medical care Joe's elderly dog requires.*

In the above example, Joe could have kept his account in his own name without designating a "pay on death" beneficiary. When Joe died, the asset (the account) would have then been subject to his Last Will document with $10,000 going to Tim for the care of Joe's dog. Allie would not have had any discretion about what would happen to those funds.

Asset title is so important. Knowing how it works really impacts what occurs upon death. I find that there are many people like Joe who simply do not understand this.

What Your Last Will and Testament Should Do

If you do a Will, it should designate who is in charge of the assets passing through the Will, who gets your assets, and when. To help with creating the Will, I ask clients to explain to me in their own words what they would like to happen and what is important in the event that they die. I then try to narrow down the issues and repeat everything back to them. The point is to have a Will document that reflects what the individual wants.

For those including their pets in their estate planning documents, the issues also include:

- Who is the Pet Custodian?
- Where should the pet go?
- Will there be any funds that follow the pet in Trust or otherwise?

Detailed options for pet planning (like Trusts) are more fully explained in Part 2 of this book.

The Executor of a Last Will and Testament

An Executor (also sometimes known as a "personal representative") is the person in a Last Will document who is nominated to be in charge of the probate proceedings after the death of the person in question. If the nominated person agrees to do the Executor job, he or she will wrap up the last legal affairs of the deceased person's life via probate. The process differs depending on the state in which the decedent lived, but the Executor usually goes to court to be appointed and receives an order from the court officially appointing him or her. An Executor is almost certainly entitled to be paid for this job.

The Executor job is often more challenging than people think. Here are some examples of what an Executor does.

An Executor determines what assets are subject to the Last Will and Testament. Since the vast majority of pets do not have title, your pet will be subject to your Will along with any other assets you own in your own name alone.

An Executor pays the last bills of the deceased person. Yes, your creditors are still there waiting, even if you die -- your last credit card bill, medical bills, cell phone, etc. all need to be paid. Your Executor notifies each creditor of your death and (if you have the assets) pays your final bills.

An Executor must wrap up the last legal details of a deceased person's life. This includes filing the last tax return; turning off the phone and utilities; closing bank accounts; closing down a person's online life (including social media); and making sure everything is out of the name of the person who died. Real estate may need to be sold.

Many people think that the job of closing up the details of a person's life will be easy. To the contrary, it can be a real challenge even if the person who died lived a simple life. Even if a person lived alone, he or she likely had a cable bill, a tax return, and so forth. Ask yourself whether it will be easy or fun to clean out someone else's garage. All of this will have to be taken care of by a person legally empowered to do so.

An Executor divides money/stock/business interests. After debts are paid and all of the legal aspects of your life are taken care of, your Executor distributes your assets to those who are legally entitled.

An Executor distributes personal property. The personal property of a person who has died will need to be gone through, disposed of, sold, or given to the beneficiaries. While it doesn't *sound* that hard, I find this to be one of the Executor's most challenging jobs. If a Last Will says, "I give all of my personal property equally to my four children," which child gets the china? The jewelry? The bedroom furniture? What if they all want those items? What if no one does? Now add a pet or pets into the mix. It can become a very difficult situation. An Executor is responsible for handling any problems connected to the estate. Fighting family members, disagreements as to who gets what, creditor issues – these all fall under an Executor's umbrella.

Choosing the Right Executor

The Executor you choose needs to be able to handle the job and be willing to do it. This may seem obvious, however in my experience, picking an Executor is not as simple as it may seem. For one thing, the person who would be an appropriate Executor right now may not be the right choice a few years from now. People change; you change. Your life and the people in it can be vastly different in the future. It is important to revisit this issue every few years.

With regard to pet estate planning, it's important that your Executor is someone who is on the same page as you. If you choose someone who thinks that planning for your pet is foolish, they may not follow your wishes. For example, imagine that your pet was standing in the way of a family member receiving money; an Executor who didn't believe in Pet Estate Planning might be inclined to disregard your Will. It's not like your pet is going to hire an attorney, although that would be awesome. No, your pet is on his/her own. You want to pick an Executor who will advocate for your pet. If you have a Pet Custodian (see below), he or she can also protect the rights of your pet.

Choosing A Pet Custodian

A Pet Custodian is a term I use to refer to the person in your documents who will take physical custody of your pet. Basically, this is the person who will be the new pet parent. For me, this is extremely important. Should something happen to my husband and me, it is important to me that the person who gets my human children also take my fur baby; my human children and fur baby need to stay together. See more on Pet Custodians in Chapter 4.

When a Person Dies Without a Last Will

Whether or not you make a plan for what happens to your assets after you die, decisions must be made. The world does not stop just because you do. That's a harsh reality. The "who is in charge" and "who gets what" issues still have to be determined. As discussed, if you haven't planned for these things, someone else will; that someone will be determined by the state laws which dictate all of those things.

When I tell people this, some react by saying that if someone else will do it, then why should I? The answer to that question is that the decisions made *for you* are often contrary to what you would have wanted. This is especially true when one of your priorities is providing for your pet family members. Here are some examples:

Layla is a woman in her sixties who rescues cats and volunteers at a local rescue dedicated to the care of animals. At any given time she has two adult cats living in her home and she fosters kittens to get them ready for adoption. Her two grown children think her interest in cats is silly and they tease her, calling her the "crazy cat lady." Layla knows this and she responds by telling them that she may be crazy but she loves cats and especially the ones that live with her. She tells her children that they had better take care of her adult cats if anything happens to her. Layla has a stroke and dies. She does not have a Will. At the funeral, one of Layla's rescue friends offers to take her adult cats. Layla's children had already put all of the cats (including the kittens) outside. One was hit by a car and died. They have not seen the others.

Contrast that example with this one:

Layla knows her children refer to her as the "crazy cat lady." Layla has a Last Will prepared and names her friend from the animal rescue center as her Pet Custodian. The two have talked about Layla's instructions. Layla has a stroke and dies. When Layla does not show up for her volunteer shift, her friend inquires and is told the sad news. Her friend brings the adult cats to her home and takes all of the fostered kittens to the rescue to be re-assigned to new homes. Layla's children are thrilled not to have to worry about those "silly" cats.

As the above examples illustrate, sometimes it is just simple planning that can make a difference in the lives of pets.

Common Excuses for Not Having a Will

I really enjoy talking to the public about estate planning and probate. It helps to get out of my lawyer mindset and have the opportunity to hear what people truly think about estate planning and probate, what their fears are, and what their friends are telling them. I hear many excuses for why a person has not completed his or her estate planning. Here are some of the most common reasons:

Lawyers (and Wills) are too expensive. Yes, *some* lawyers are too expensive, there is no doubt about that. However, the right lawyer is one that charges you a fair price, gets the work done, and does not draft documents that include provisions that benefit himself or herself. But guess what? It's not going to be free.

Even though I love a good bargain, there is a place for getting a good deal, such as buying the generic brand over a name brand; estate planning is not the same. I know it seems self-serving, but estate planning is not an area where you should cut corners or go for a "deal." The adage "you get what you pay for," in my opinion, is never more true than here.

How your estate plan is drafted is important. Not only will it be a permanent record, it may mean the difference between your pet being re-homed as you would want and ending up with someone who doesn't want him/her. It may mean a smooth transition for your beloved fur baby versus one that is rough. Careful drafting ensures that your documents address the issues that are important to you.

Estate planning is too complicated. Yes, it's complicated, and dying is as well. I wish we did not have to do it. Yet, we do. A qualified estate planning lawyer who does this type of work for a living should make it as easy as possible by:

- providing you with only the documents that you need;
- explaining those documents and then summarizing them in writing;
- drafting the documents to reflect your wishes, including providing for your fur babies if that is what you want;
- reviewing your situation to make the documents specific to you; and
- ethically performing the work for a fair price.

My family can take care of it when I die. When people say this to me, I have a mental vision of someone scooping piles of their money into a fireplace and laughing an evil cartoonish laugh. An exaggeration, but my point is that yes, someone will indeed "work it out," but he or she will likely have to jump through many more hoops, and it will take more time and cost more than if the person simply took care of business before death.

I do not have enough assets to need estate planning. Estate planning is not just for the wealthy. To the contrary, if you have any assets at all in your own name, then someone will need to begin the process of having those assets transferred upon your death, which may mean probate. An asset can be anything from your bank account to your car. It can even include your furniture. What's more, these tasks need to be completed even if you have a great deal of debt. And those with modest means still probably have a last tax return to be filed, a car to be sold, insurance premiums to be cancelled, and so forth.

For those with pets, estate planning can have an impact. Issues like who takes them and who will watch out for them have to be resolved. Failing to put a plan in place means leaving these important decisions to chance.

My creditors will get everything, so why should I care about estate planning? If you die with a lot of debt, it is not necessarily true that your creditors will get everything. Visa does not want your dog (although, if they met mine, they might!). In many states, if you die and there is a surviving spouse or children, there is an amount that the spouse or children may be entitled to *before* creditors can take your assets. This could mean that your stuff—or even money—can go to your loved ones even if there are substantial debts. Also, typically the person in charge of your estate may be entitled to a fee *before* a creditor gets paid. While you may think that what you have is not much, to those you leave behind, a little can be a lot.

I will complete my estate planning when it is time. If you are alive and age eighteen or older with assets, it's time. Sometimes I am asked to go to a hospital with a Last Will and Testament document for someone to sign who is near death. While I appreciate that sometimes, we as humans do not want to face the reality of death until there is absolutely no hope, waiting until the last minute creates a difficult estate planning situation. It is essentially "crisis management." It costs more and has a lot more risk for everyone. I am generally not inclined to participate in this. Sometimes, people just wait too long. If there is a serious medical event and they are too impaired or there is substantial pain medication, there is an issue as to whether a person can and should really be making serious legal decisions.

I cannot make the hard decisions necessary for a Will. My clients struggle with the same decisions that I do regarding estate planning documents, including the following:

- Who is the right person to be in charge?
- Who should be the guardian of my minor children?
- Who should handle the money for my kids until they grown up?
- Who should take my pet?
- Should I designate an amount to be kept with the pet?
- How do I leave assets?

These can be difficult questions. The suggestion I give to my clients is to just make the best decision you can at this point in time. I see many situations where a person dies without a Last Will and Testament and the resulting chaos is damaging to the family. It would have been better if the person who passed away had just done the best he or she could and made decisions.

Summary for Planning for Your Death

- Not all assets pass under your Will.
- Title to assets dictates how they are distributed at your death.
- Decide on an Executor (the person you designate under your Last Will to be in charge of your probate).
- Decide on an alternate Executor (in case the one you appoint cannot act).
- Decide on a Pet Custodian.
- Decide on an alternate Pet Custodian (in case the one you appoint cannot act).
- Have a conversation with the Pet Custodian about the specifics and his or her willingness to act.

- If your Pet Custodian is *not* the same person as the person who will be your Executor, make sure that your Executor is aware of the Pet Custodian.
- Locate an estate planning attorney who will draft the documents with the above in mind.

Part Two

Pet Estate Planning In Depth

CHAPTER 4

Pet Trusts

A Trust is a fancy kind of a thing, or at least that is the public perception. When people hear "Trust," many automatically think "trust fund baby," assuming that a Trust is only for the children of the very, very rich – the ones who sit around and wait for their check to be deposited before sleeping until noon, shopping, and then hitting the bar scene. Yes, there are definitely a few of those around, and yes, I have met more than my fair share of them. However, Trusts are not just for the wealthy. While Trusts certainly are part of the estate planning process for those with wealth, anyone of just about any means can use them to place restrictions on how money or other assets are to be distributed, even to a pet.

This chapter focuses specifically on Pet Trusts as a vehicle for estate planning. Learning what a Trust is and what it can do can be somewhat complicated. However, for those that want to explore setting aside money for their pets and set up parameters for the use of those funds, this chapter provides you with the information needed to determine if a Pet Trust is right for you.

Trusts: the Basics

When clients express to me that they want to provide for a pet in their estate planning, I ask them to tell me what they want to happen and then I do what I can to make the documents a reality. Some clients want very simple provisions, such as: "I give my cat, Muffin, to my sister." On the other hand, some clients have a very detailed plan in mind that includes setting aside money specifically for the pet so that the pet can be taken care of in a way that the client dictates. For those more complex situations, a trust can provide the solution.

Trust Defined

My definition of a Trust is a relationship under law where one person or entity holds property (any kind of assets or money) and designates another person to be in charge of it under certain defined terms and conditions. A Trust can be drafted to suit your specific needs under most circumstances.

Types of Trusts

Estate planning attorneys have different types of Trusts at their disposal. When and how to use them has to do with the situation at hand. For our purposes, here are some facts about Trusts:

- A Trust can be established within a Last Will and Testament document.
- A Trust can be established outside of a Last Will and Testament document as a freestanding entity that can still receive assets from a Last Will and Testament document after someone dies.
- Trusts can be revocable (changeable) or irrevocable (harder to change, although, many times, not impossible).

The Trusts I draft for clients' pets are normally found inside of a Last Will document, or they're revocable, and therefore can be changed during the life of the person who made them.

Creating a Pet Trust

Many states have real and true laws on the books that specifically allow you to have a Trust for your pet. This "Pet Trust" is an arrangement that allows money or assets to be set aside for certain uses related to your pet or pets.

A Pet Trust, like other Trusts, is a legal entity once it becomes active. It has a Trustee, a person who is legally in charge of it, and it has a beneficiary, the pet, who is entitled to use of the funds in the way that the Pet Trust specifically provides.

Here's how a Pet Trust is formed, at a basic level: a person hires an attorney to draft estate planning documents that contain language leaving property or money in a Trust for the benefit of a pet or pets, the terms of which are housed inside the estate planning documents (like a Last Will and Testament or a Revocable Trust), and he or she designates who is in charge. This is an example of a Trust formation provision that might be found in a Will:

> If at the time of my death, my dog, Holly, is then living, then:
>
> (1) I give and bequeath Holly to my Friend, Lindsey, who shall be Holly's Pet Custodian; and
> (2) I give and bequeath the sum of fifty thousand (50,000) dollars to the Trustee of the "Holly: Best Dog Ever Trust" to be held, administered, and distributed in accordance with ITEM X of this my Last Will and Testament. Provided, however, if at the time of my death, my dog, Holly, is not then living, then this gift is void.

The result is that if at the time of the person's death, Holly was alive and, assuming the person had $50,000 to pass through his/her Will, then $50,000 would go to the Trustee of the "Holly: Best Dog Ever Trust." The actual Trust provisions, found in ITEM X, could be simple or complex; they would dictate how the money was used. In the event of death, the Executor would give Holly to the Pet Custodian and also $50,000 of the assets to the named Trustee of the Pet Trust.

In this example, Holly's Trust is inside a Will document, but it could have been in a free-standing Trust document separate from a Will. A Will is generally a document that is open to the public for viewing after you die. Placing a Pet Trust inside a free-standing Trust document that is separate from your Will can provide a privacy element and that can be important if, for example, you have people in your life that would oppose estate planning for your pets (see Chapter 7: When Family Members Are Opposed to Pet Estate Planning).

Pet Trust Provisions

While you are alive and you have capacity, you own your pet - you control the care, feeding, and decisions. All is right with the world. The benefit of establishing a Pet Trust is that if you are dead or cannot act for yourself, the money you set aside in your Pet Trust will be used for your pet in a manner that you dictate.

This means that before spelling out specific provisions in your Pet Trust, you should contemplate what you want for your pet – what their particular needs are – and include them within the document. A well-drafted Pet Trust should do the following:

- establish rights for your pet and define the proper use of funds including distributions to the Pet Custodian (the person who has physical custody of your pet)
- designate a Pet Trustee (the person or entity in charge of money)
- designate a Pet Custodian
- say what happens to any leftover funds when the pet dies

Your Pet's Rights and Proper Use of Funds

Language is often included in a Pet Trust that allows a Pet Trustee to distribute any amount of Trust assets in his/her "absolute discretion" for the "support" of the pet beneficiary. This is appropriate when your Pet Trustee and Pet Custodian are reliable people. However, it is always a good idea to specifically provide for the proper use of Pet Trust funds.

Consider what you would like your Pet Trust to do. In the Pet Trusts that I have prepared, the most common provisions indicate that funds can be used for any and all of the following:

- medical care (vaccinations, check-ups, dental care)
- grooming
- daycare
- food
- toys
- dog park fees
- other general pet-related costs (examples: bags for cleaning up poop or kitty litter)

The use of the funds can be general or it can be very limited. Preferences are pet-parent specific.

Distributions to a Pet Custodian

You can also allocate funds to your Pet Custodian in consideration of his/her taking in your fur baby – something outside of what you might leave for care and feeding costs. You may have gotten the cute baby animal years; now that you cannot care for your precious one, the Pet Custodian is getting a full-grown pet that perhaps has medical issues. Even if he/she is an animal lover, it takes time and effort to take care of any pet. Maybe not the greatest deal, so it's possible for you to compensate your Pet Custodian with money. For example, you may indicate that if your pet is living at the time of your death, and the Pet Custodian agrees to take your pet, he or she would receive a gift. The how much is up to you.

The Last Illness and Death of your Pet

In your Trust, you have the option to indicate whether funds can be used for your pet's last illness. We all know that the lifespan of a common pet is typically much less than humans. Sometimes pets will have medical conditions which we treat in the hopes of recovery. When we do all we can, though, and it's time for the pet to pass, your Pet Trust can also cover the cost of the burial. Here's an example of language:

> If my dog, CAMMIE, dies prior to complete distribu-
> tion of the principal of her Trust, the Trustee may, in
> the Trustee's discretion, pay from her Trust the expenses
> of her last illness, the costs of burial at a pet cemetery,
> and related expenses.

I find that directives such as this make it easier on the Trustee and the Pet Custodian because all parties know what is expected. See Chapter 5: Pet Burials for more on this subject.

Compassionate Death. The thought of "putting down" a pet…well, it's just awful. It's so hard to think about. Yet, I know that when a pet is in a great deal of pain and medical treatment cannot help, it becomes necessary to consider allowing a compassionate end-of-life plan. In my Pet Trust, I address this delicate topic. I want to make sure that my Pet Custodian knows that while I do not expect miracles, I do want compassion. Here's an example of the language that I have used in Pet Trusts about this difficult subject:

> The Pet Custodian has the authority to euthanize my dog, CAMMIE, after first determining from a licensed veterinarian that condition, injury, or disease of CAMMIE will substantially impair the quality of life of CAMMIE. When evaluating CAMMIE's quality of life, I direct that my Pet Custodian consider all factors including her comfort, whether she has life-threatening injuries or a terminal illness which is causing significant discomfort, and her age.

Leftover Funds. Your Pet Trust needs to say what happens to any remaining funds when your pet dies. Usually I recommend that clients designate a charity rather than a person or family member. If you name a family member, then they actually benefit from your pet dying. He or she may, for example, not be so excited for medical treatments because the result would be that he or she gets less. That's usually not the ideal situation. Contrast that with a charity dedicated to animals that receives the funds after your pet dies; they usually are just grateful for the funds. Here's an example:

> *Sam is unmarried with an adult son, Logan. Sam has a cat, Boots, that he adores. Logan tolerates Boots, but cats are not his favorite and it drives him crazy that his dad loves the cat so much. Sam's estate planning documents leave all of his assets ($40,000) in a Pet Trust for Boots with Logan as the Trustee. The Pet Trust says that when Boots dies Logan gets the money that is left, but he cannot get it until Boots dies. Boots is eleven years old when Sam dies. Sam's neighbor, Kylie, is the Pet Custodian for Boots. A year after Sam dies, Kylie reaches out to Logan about some medical bills for Boots. Logan tells Kylie that he never put the money in a Trust for Boots because "that's stupid" and he spent the money on a truck which he then wrecked.*

In the above example, Logan was not a good choice to be the Pet Trustee for the funds set aside for Boots. Sam should have known better, but as human beings sometimes we just believe that those we love will do the right thing. Here's how that situation could have been different:

> *Sam's estate planning documents leave half of his assets ($20,000) in a Pet Trust for Boots with his neighbor Kylie as the Trustee and the Pet Custodian. Logan gets the other half. The Pet Trust says that when Boots dies an animal charity gets whatever is left. Boots is loved by Kylie and has a good life. Logan gets his money right away and is happy; he does not bother Kylie about the Pet Trust because he knows he is not getting the money. Five years after Sam dies, Boots dies. Kylie terminates the Pet Trust and gives the remaining money to the charity designated in the Pet Trust.*

In the second scenario, Boots gets a home, Kylie gets the use of Sam's funds, and Logan gets an inheritance. This result was made possible because Sam had the document in place, picked the right people to be in charge, and made good choices about the distribution of the money.

Designate a Pet Trustee

A Trustee is the person who is legally responsible for managing all aspects of a Trust. When the Pet Trust comes into existence, the terms, restrictions, and provisions are set and dictate where each asset subject to the Trust must go. This is a big deal because it means that the Trustee is the person in charge of the Trust assets. From a practical standpoint, a Trustee must:

- set up a Trust financial account to hold the assets
- invest Trust assets (for example: cash, stocks, money market accounts, etc.)
- manage the Trust assets (for example, if the Trust includes real estate)
- make distributions in accordance with the Trust terms
- get a tax ID number
- file taxes (if required each year)

Here's an example:

> Susan is married to a man named Lee, her second husband.
> Susan has a cat, Belle, who she adores and who she had be-
> fore she married Lee. Lee doesn't like Belle and is allergic.
> Susan's estate planning documents leave 90% of her assets
> outright to Lee and 10% in a Pet Trust for Belle. Susan
> names her friend, Robert, as the Trustee of her Trust. Su-
> san's neighbor, Valerie, is the Pet Custodian for Belle.
> When Susan dies, the amount going into the Pet Trust is
> $20,000. Robert takes the $20,000 check and opens up a
> money market account at a local bank. Robert communi-
> cates with Valerie about the monthly care and costs for
> Belle. When Belle dies, Robert closes the bank account and,
> as required under Susan's Pet Trust, gives the remaining
> money to a designated local charity.

In the above example, after Susan dies the significant participants are:

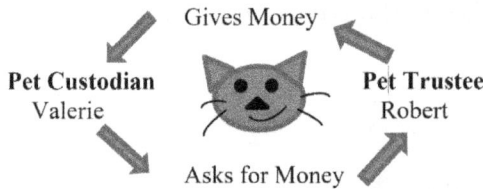

The Pet Trustee took charge of the money and worked with the Pet Custodian, who asked for funds when necessary for Belle's care.

Pet Trustee Options

In my experience the best Trustees are the ones who meet these requirements: they're willing to do the job; are at least somewhat sophisticated
when it comes to business; will take a fair and reasonable fee; will abide by
the Pet Trust provisions; and will not take advantage of the situation by
using the Pet Trust fund for themselves. A Pet Trust Trustee should view
the Trust as an extension of your wishes and take the role seriously.

In choosing a Pet Trustee your options are generally: a friend or family member; a bank or trust company; or another type of professional (for instance an attorney or CPA). What's important to making a good choice is knowledge that a Trustee will be legally in charge, which means that he or she will have access to the Trust assets and control over complying with your Pet Trust provisions.

A Friend or Family Member. Generally, I think that most of us can rattle off the top of our heads the people we know who would be good at handling money for us. I know I can. When I think of suitable candidates, I think of those people I know who are smart with money, trustworthy, who like me enough to do the Trustee job, and who would not take advantage of the situation. If you have that person in your life, name them as your Pet Trustee and also name an alternate.

It can be hard to know who to pick – maybe you have someone in mind who is fantastic with money but is negative about creating a Pet Trust, or perhaps you have someone you think would be great, but they are very young. If you want to choose a specific person but have reservations about his or her abilities or about whether he/she will do the job effectively, here are some options:

1) Talk with the person about it. If you are like me, you have people in your life that you just trust. You would hand them your most prized possession and leave for two years and when you came back it would be in the same shape it was in when you left. Even though I hope you have at least one of these people around, he or she may not be excited about being a Trustee of a Pet Trust and you need to know that up front. There can be a full range of responses – they could be supportive and want to do it, negative about it, or otherwise. In any event, you will have some idea as to whether this is the right person for the job.

2) Name more than one person to act together as Co-Trustees. Two people doing one job can be a hassle because it means that they have to agree on decisions. However, it also means that there are two sets of eyes on your money in the Pet Trust. Having two people might be a good idea if, for example, you have a person that is qualified to be the Pet Trustee, but they are young or elderly. Hav-

ing an additional person can also mean that the job gets done more effectively because the strengths of two are applied to the tasks.

3) Name a good alternate. If the person you pick cannot do the job or they die or become incapacitated, it's important to have another Trustee in place who can step up and do the job.

A Bank or Trust Company. Many banks have trust departments whose business is to administer Trusts. In most situations, I very much like a bank or trust company as a Trustee for larger amounts of money or complicated assets. They tend to do a very good job because they are designed to invest Trust assets, follow the rules of the Trust, treat the situation objectively, and follow all tax-reporting rules. Generally speaking, your Trust assets and your beneficiaries are in very good hands.

Ah, but like every option, there are drawbacks. With professional Trustees, the drawback is the Trustee fee charged. Getting great service in an all-in-one location comes with a price tag. For those with significant assets, it's worth it, but for those with assets that are not large, having a professional Trustee is just not cost efficient. This is not a secret, and the banks and trust companies that I encounter are upfront about this. Where I live, for example, in my opinion if you have anything less than about $300,000 in Trust, it's not cost effective to have a professional Trustee.

I have also discovered that some banks and trust companies are reluctant to be Pet Trustees. This baffles me. You can make my dog happy by just giving her one (one!) extra treat. Compare that to a human teenager trust-fund baby! A pet is much easier.

Other professionals. There are Trustee options other than a friend, family member, bank, or trust company. For example, you could enlist a lawyer, financial planner, insurance agent, or accountant. Generally, my opinion is that unless this professional is related to you by blood, marriage, or adoption, I am not inclined to like this option in most situations. The reason is that many times, in my experience, these people simply do not do a good job. The expression "jack of all trades and master of none" comes to mind.

Your CPA may be bright and capable, but he or she likely has no idea what the Trust laws in your state say. Further, he or she may not have any idea how to administer a Trust. Compare this with an actual trust company that has a team involved and that team includes an investment person, a lawyer who knows the Trust laws, an accountant, and a person whose job it is to make sure your beneficiary is being provided for as required under your Trust document. For me there is no comparison.

After your death or incapacity, once a non-trust company "professional" is in place as a Trustee, there is a risk that he or she will stay no matter what the quality of his or her job performance. Getting this person to agree to resign is typically very difficult. What I have found is that sometimes a lawyer, for example, will consider your Trust an annuity stream (to themselves!). They do very little and charge a fee to the Trust monthly or annually. And as you may have guessed, these people do not want to give up this easy money; what's more, since you are dead or incapacitated, it can be hard to make them leave. Here's an example:

Kyle rescues special needs animals. He has funds set aside in a bank account to take care of any animals in his possession at the time of his death. His neighbor has a son who is an attorney. Kyle goes to see him and tells the attorney that he wants to make sure that the funds he has saved are "legal" for his pets. The attorney tells Kyle that he will make sure his pets are taken care of and drafts a Will document that requires Kyle's money to be placed into a Pet Trust with the attorney in charge. Kyle later dies and the money in the account, $100,000, is placed in the Trust. The lawyer neglected to arrange for a Pet Custodian in Kyle's Will. The lawyer buys cheap cages and puts the special needs animals in those cages in his mom's back yard. Kyle's friends are furious to learn of the situation, but they cannot afford to hire an attorney to fight for Kyle's animals. The attorney takes a fee of $25,000 a year. He spends little on the animals, most of whom die in the next year. In three years, all of Kyle's animals are dead and the lawyer received almost 100% of Kyle's money.

While this is a very extreme example, it goes to show you the importance of quality within your plan. Having the right Pet Custodian means that your fur babies will have an advocate.

Escape Hatches That Apply to Trustees

No matter who you decide should be your Pet Trustee, including the right provisions within the Trust document means that if something goes wrong (if there's financial abuse, for example), there is an avenue for dealing with it.

I like to make sure there are "escape hatches" in almost every Trust document I draft for clients. These escape hatches allow certain people, like your Pet Custodian, to force the resignation of a poor-quality Pet Trustee by just doing things like giving them written notice and appointing a new (and qualified) Trustee.

Here are examples of "escape hatches" that I sometimes employ:

<u>Have provisions that are specific to your pet</u>. For example: "This trust can pay for boarding when necessary, daycare, all vet visits, food, toys, and illness."

<u>Allow the Pet Custodian to see annual accountings</u>. This means that the person handling the money has to show the Pet Custodian what he or she is doing at least once a year. If the Trustee knows someone is looking, it keeps them accountable.

<u>Allow the Pet Custodian or another person to remove the Trustee for certain violations</u>. Things like failing to give money or account for assets should be removable offenses. Indicate how the Trustee can be fired, who makes that decision, and who the alternate will be.

<u>Limit the fee of the Trustee inside the Trust document</u>. One aspect of Trustee work that drives me crazy is when a Trustee is caught doing something wrong but nonetheless refuses to leave and then hires a team of lawyers and has the Trust assets pay for those lawyers. This is so frustrating. What is surprising to most people is that even if a Trustee takes money, there is often no criminal punishment. None. I am told that the rationale behind this is that it's a civil (financial), not a criminal matter. Truthfully, I can sometimes see why. For example, if you

named your attorney, Richard, as your Trustee and after you die he takes $10,000 a year as a "fee," you and I may agree that this is too much and contrary to your intent. But in our example, you would be dead and Richard may claim to the authorities, to your Pet Custodian, or to anyone who asks that this is what you wanted.

If it's not written down, those looking at the situation cannot know what you wanted. Fighting it out in court can be expensive and then it becomes a case of "he said, she said." If your estate planning documents spell out the rules, then a lot of chaos and confusion can be avoided.

Name a "Special Trustee." Another option is to name a "Special Trustee" that any party involved with your Pet can contact is something goes wrong. This should be someone independent (of the Pet Trustee, Pet Custodian, and others) who could, for example report to the Court things like abuse of your Pet or financial wrongdoing. The very act of naming this person could keep all parties accountable.

Bonding. Another option is to require that the Trustee be "bonded." Basically, this requires the Trustee to purchase an insurance product that will pay if wrongdoing occurs. These bonds are sold by insurance agents and usually require an annual premium to be paid. The premium is a Trust expense. Most of the time my clients like to avoid doing a bond but it can be useful to make the other individuals involved with the Trust feel better about a Trustee that they do not agree is the best choice.

Hiring a Trust Professional or Entity

If you do choose to appoint a bank, trust company, or a professional as your trustee, here are some tips for choosing the right one for you:

Research and Interview. Conduct good research on this professional or entity. Do not just rely on one meeting; do an interview and ask if this person (representing themselves or an entity) would be willing to sign an agreement whereby his or her obligations would be spelled out and the fee would be a sum based on a scale of services provided. Put that agreement with your estate planning documents.

<u>Choose Someone Who's on the Same Page.</u> Probably the most important factor in hiring a Trustee is that the person or entity you choose should respect that the Trust funds are for your pet. There are plenty of people who would deem allocating money to a pet silly; you do not want one of those people in charge. Being a Trustee is a job, and the person or entity you pick should be onboard with performing that job in a way that reflects your wishes.

Designate a Pet Custodian

A Pet Custodian is not a janitor for your pets (that's a joke folks). As discussed, it's a person appointed in your estate planning documents to be in charge of your pet or pets if you die or become incapacitated. When parents come to me and have human children, we designate a "guardian" for minors in the event the parents are deceased. Designating a Pet Custodian is the same concept. Basically, they take your pets if you cannot care for them anymore.

Choosing your Pet Custodian

Although I am not aware that any state has an actual legal designation of "Pet Custodian," my opinion is that you could nonetheless designate such a person in your estate planning documents. I do so in my own documents.

My preference is to name a Pet Custodian and also to name an alternate Pet Custodian. In other words, I have a number one draft pick but if that does not work out, I have a number two named as well.

Putting your Pet Custodian in your Estate Planning Documents

A Pet Custodian should be in almost all of your estate planning documents. It should be in the documents that may be used while you are alive (like a Power of Attorney) and then when you die (like your Will or Revocable Trust).

Here is an example of what a Pet Custodian designation could look like in a Last Will and Testament that is specific to one pet:

> <u>Pet Custodian.</u> In the event of my death, if my cat, Muffin, is then living, then I give and bequeath Muffin

to my sister, Kristine. Provided however, if at the time of my death, Kristine cannot or will not take Muffin, then I give and bequeath Muffin to my neighbor, Lindsay. Provided, further, if Lindsay cannot or will not take Muffin, then I direct that my Executor shall find a loving home for Muffin. Provided, finally, if Muffin is not living at the time of my death, then this gift shall be void.

Here is an example of what a Pet Custodian designation could look like in a Last Testament that is general and can apply to any pet owned at your death:

> Pet Custodian. In the event of my death, if I own any pets including but not limited to dogs, cats, horses, goats, birds, rodents, etc., then I give and bequeath all pets in the home that are then living to my sister, Kristine. Provided however, if at the time of my death, Kristine cannot or will not take my pets that were in my home, then I give and bequeath my pets to my neighbor, Lindsay. Provided, further, if Lindsay cannot or will not take my home pets, then I direct that my Executor shall find loving homes for all. With regard to my outside pets such as horses and goats, I give and bequeath those pets to my friend, Ben, who I feel confident has the ability and space to provide a happy environment. Provided, if Ben, cannot or will not take my outside pets, then I ask Ben to find suitable homes for all.

Information for your Pet Custodian

Although my human children cannot yet do things like vote, enter into contracts, or live on their own, they can talk. If something happened to both my husband and I, my children could tell you what they like to eat, where they go to school, and what sports they play. Your fur babies cannot talk. If suddenly you were not able to be around in the way you are now, consider what information a Pet Custodian would need about the care of your fur baby or babies. Be specific. Here's a list of some information that may be relevant:

- Location of medical records
- Preferred veterinarian
- Medications (type and when and how to give)
- Allergies
- Food types
- Food amounts
- Frequency and type of treats
- Contact information for groomer and normal grooming schedule
- Normal schedule (example, three walks a day)
- Issues (things like "nips at small children" are good to know)

This information does not have to be in your estate planning documents -- it can be written on paper or even emailed to your Pet Custodian after you inquire whether this person would do the job for you in the event he or she is called upon. The important aspect is that it is done. Your pets love you and if something happens to you, planning ahead will make it easier on them.

Funding a Pet Trust

Many times, clients just rely upon whatever pot of assets they have at death to fund a Pet Trust. However, the reality is that just about any asset can be made a part of a Trust – bank accounts, investment accounts, real estate, royalty interests, etc. For example, a Last Will could provide that ten percent of all assets go into your Pet Trust for a pet and at death, the ten percent is determined by looking at all of the assets that are passing through the Will.

Some clients will designate their Trust as the beneficiary of a life insurance or retirement policy so there is a known source of funding for the Pet Trust and a specific amount. For example, a client could name a spouse as the first beneficiary of a life insurance policy for $25,000 and the secondary beneficiary (if the spouse was deceased) as:

The Smith Pet Trust established in the Last Will and Testament of Lilly Smith dated October 24, 2017.

The result would be that if Lilly Smith died and her husband was not alive, her Pet Trust would receive the check in the amount of $25,000 and the funds would be used as the Smith Pet Trust provisions required.

The important part is to have some idea of what will be passing to the Pet Trust.

Common Questions About Pet Trusts

How do Trust assets get into a Pet Trust? The answer depends upon what type of Trust it is. In a Revocable or Irrevocable Trust outside of a Will, assets might already be in there when the pet parent dies because the owner transferred the asset to the Trust. For example, if you have a Revocable Trust, then you could go to your bank and ask them to title your checking account into your Revocable Trust. Assuming the account existed when you died, the asset would already be in your Trust. Whereas, for a Trust in a Will, the assets typically pass through probate *after* the pet parent dies and then goes into the Trust. When a client names a Trust as the beneficiary of a life insurance policy or retirement account, then a check is made payable in the name of the Trust and the Trustee deposits it into an account which is titled in the name of the Trust.

Who is in charge of a Pet Trust? A "Pet Trustee" is a person who becomes in charge of the Trust assets and has to do things like manage the trust money, file taxes, and distribute money in accordance with the terms of the Trust. Usually the controlling document appoints the Trustee and then an alternate Trustee if the first person or entity cannot act.

Does a Trustee get paid? Yes, they can be paid. Some states have set amounts while others just say the amount must be "reasonable." Some states allow the person creating the Trust to dictate payment.

What if the pet dies? A Pet Trust would say within the document what happens when the pet or pets die. Usually, the Pet Trust terminates and the funds are given to a specified person or charity.

What if I have more than one pet? It depends upon state law, but mostly it is fine to have a Pet Trust that is for more than one pet.

What if I have exotic Pets? It depends upon state law, but probably fine. See Chapter 6.

What if my number of pets changes before death? A good attorney will draft a document that takes this into consideration. So, for example, the Pet Trust may be established for "all pets that I have at the time of my death." This makes it very flexible.

How long can a Pet Trust last? Many states have laws that say but generally, for the life of the longest living pet who is a beneficiary.

Can I name my Pet Trust anything I want? Pretty much. I mean, I would rule out calling it anything profane but other than that I think you have a lot of freedom. Most of my clients tend to call it the family surname followed by the term "Pet Trust." Thus, for example, a client may choose to call his or her Pet Trust the "Smith Family Pet Trust." However, some people like to have a little fun or pay tribute with the name. In my documents, the Pet Trust for my fur baby is called the "Holly Best Dog Ever Trust."

Where are the provisions of a Trust actually located? A Trust can be established within a Last Will and Testament document; outside of a Last Will document as a freestanding entity that can still receive assets from a Last Will document after someone dies; or inside another Trust like a Revocable Living Trust.

Can a Trust be changed? Trusts can be revocable (changeable) or irrevocable (harder to change, although many times, not impossible). If a Trust is inside of a Last Will and Testament document, then it can be changed if and when the Last Will document is changed. The same is true for a Revocable Trust when the person who created it is still alive and has the capacity to change it.

When a person dies or if a person becomes incapacitated, then with few exceptions, a Last Will and a Trust cannot be changed.

A Pet Trust is Not for Everyone: Other Options

Having a Pet Trust and finding a lawyer to do it can be daunting and the truth is some people simply do not have the means to do it. You can have very little in the way of money and assets but still have the desire to take care of your pets in the event something happens to you. For pet parents who are not able or willing to take the leap into a full-on estate plan that includes a Pet Trust, here are some basics options that might assist you:

- Choose a Pet Custodian and an alternate in your Last Will and inquire as to whether they would do the job.
- Make it clear who should have your pets if you get sick or die and write it down.
- Write down all of the information necessary about your pets.
- Re-title a small bank account such that your Pet Custodian will get the money when you die. For example, a "pay on death" designation. But note that doing this means they would get the money if the account was titled this way at death even if they rejected your pet or your pet died before you. Consider this carefully.

Pet Trust Checklist

- Determine whether you would like to appoint a Pet Custodian
- Determine who should be the Trustee
- Determine what the Pet Trust assets will be used for including but not limited to:
  - Medical Care
  - Doggie daycare
  - Food
  - Bathroom supplies (kitty litter or poop bags)
  - Grooming
  - Last illness
  - Burial
- Determine other provisions in your Trust:
  - Removal of Trustee (for certain acts)
  - Payment of Trustee (limited to a certain amount)
  - Payment to Pet Custodian (if any)
- Have a conversation with the Pet Custodian about the specifics and his or her willingness to act

- Locate a qualified estate planning attorney who will draft the documents with the above in mind

CHAPTER 5

In Tribute: Pets That Passed Away Before You

A friend of mine had a beloved big and gentle dog that passed away some years ago. I once asked him if he would get another dog. He responded that the death of his dog was too painful and he would not want to go through it again. That's understandable; when a pet passes away, for many it can be similar to the loss of a family member. I can name for you every pet that I have ever had and I know firsthand that the love for pets is real.

Our lives are different because of our pets, and life changes when they pass away. In my life, I get up with our dog. I walk her and feed her every morning. She sits next to me while I write and enjoy my coffee. We have a routine. Since we most often outlive our pets and may have several during our lifetimes, some people want to acknowledge the pet family members that passed before us.

There are countless ways to pay tribute to the pets that we lost; this chapter explores a few ideas.

"In Lieu of Flowers" Designation

Some people request that if they pass away, that "in lieu of flowers," friends and family donate to a certain charitable organization; if you'd like, you can arrange for donations to go to a pet charity in memory of a pet who died while you were alive. I think that is a fantastic idea. To do so, you may want to do the following:

- Choose your pet charity.
- Tell your important people (your Executor) that you want an in lieu of flowers designation and indicate that this would be in memory of a certain pet (or pets) that was part of your life.
- If you pre-planned your funeral, ask that the funeral home place a comment on the website designating your charity and your wish for "in lieu of flowers" to your designated organization or organizations.
- If you are one of the few that write his or her own obituaries, include an "in lieu of flowers" line, along with your designated organization or organizations, in the document.

Animal Charities: a Wealth of Choices

There are so many fine animal organizations out there; I am a huge fan of those dedicated to rescuing and also those that train pets to help humans live a better life. For example, certain groups train pets to assist veterans or children with particular medical conditions. There are also places that train dogs to sniff out bombs, drugs, or bodies, and groups that train horses, cats, and other animals to be therapy animals for people who benefit from a warm and fuzzy presence.

I follow many of these entities, and the videos and pictures pretty much make me want to empty my bank account. I cannot do so because I have responsibilities in my life; however, I can give charitably to the organizations that I like best, and I can (and I do) certainly make provisions for animal groups in my own estate planning.

Here are some tips for finding organizations that you may want to provide for in your estate planning documents:

Research Charitable Organizations. If you would like to allocate assets to a charity for animals, it is important to do your research. Make sure it's a real organization and not a scam. It's sad that this is even an issue, yet it does occur; unfortunately, certain groups/individuals take advantage of good-hearted people. Some things you can do to check on an organization:

- Search online for "reviews" and follow the charity on social media to get a feel for what they put out into the internet universe.

- If you live close by, go and visit! Arrange for a tour and volunteer if you can.
- Retain your boundaries in the relationship. I do not like it when I hear from clients that people from a charity came to their home to ask for money.
- If you cannot get up close and personal with the organization, check your state's Secretary of State website to see if the charity is registered.
- For an organization with gross receipts of more than $200,000, look for their IRS Form 990 online; this is the document these tax-exempt charities are required to file with the IRS that shows how much money comes in per year and how much is spent on things like salaries.
- Any time you name a charity to receive assets from you, make sure you check its correct legal name. (If your Secretary of State's page has a list of registered companies, per above, you can also check the correct name there.) There are some scammers out there in the world that purposely have a name similar to another charity in the hopes that they will benefit from a person who does not pay attention to detail. You can also ask for their Tax ID number. If you specify the exact legal name, a current address, and a Tax ID, you can avoid any confusion.
- Ask questions that may be important to you, such as:
  - How long have you been in business?
  - Are you a 501(c)(3) charitable organization?
  - How much of the donated money is spent on administrative costs?
  - What is your policy concerning euthanizing animals?
  - Does the organization house animals and what are the policies?

If an organization is legitimate, they depend on charitable contributions to sustain the day-to-day operations and giving either during your life or at your death can really make a difference.

Ways to Make a Charitable Gift. There are so many ways to give charitably to an animal organization, ranging from the simple to the more complicated. Here are some options:

An outright gift in the name of your pet. You can give money to a charitable animal organization in the name of your pet that has passed on. You can do this during your lifetime and get to enjoy the feeling that comes with helping animals; for example, you might see your support allow an organization to train a dog for a person with a disability. In addition, you may get a tax benefit. Win-win.

You could also place gifts in your estate planning documents which would be made upon your death. These gifts typically take one of two forms: a specific amount or a percentage of your estate.

A specific-amount gift could look like this:

I give and bequeath TEN THOUSAND DOLLARS ($10,000.00) to the XXX Shelter for Cats currently located at 111 Meeting Street, Your Town, Your State, Tax ID xxx, or its successor organization, to be used for the charitable purposes for which it was established. This gift is in memory of my cat, Milo, who brought me great joy. In the event that this organization is not in existence at the time of my death then my Executor shall give this amount to a cat charity in my home state that benefits the lives of cats.

A percentage gift could look like this:

Upon my death, my Executor shall divide my residuary assets as follows:

(A) I give, devise, and bequeath ten percent (10%) of my residuary assets to the XXX Shelter for Cats currently located at 111 Meeting Street, Your Town, Your State, Tax ID xxx, or its successor organization, to be used for the charitable purposes for which it was established. This is in memory of my cat, Milo, who brought me great joy. In the event that this organization is not in existence at the time of my death then my Executor shall give this amount to a cat charity in my home state that benefits the lives of cats.

(B) I give, devise, and bequeath the remaining ninety percent (90%) of my residuary assets to…

Naming a Charity as a Beneficiary. Some people are not aware that you can designate a charity as the beneficiary of a life insurance or retirement policy by just naming the charity on the beneficiary designation form. Another option is to name a charity as a "transfer on death" beneficiary on an account. This is usually available for assets like bank accounts or CDs. Generally, when assets pass via a beneficiary form or "transfer on death," all the charity needs is your death certificate and the funds will be immediately issued. That makes it easy and quick.

Sponsorship. Some charities allow you to become a sponsor of an animal or event in your name or in the name of your pet. For example, a local animal rescue organization may allow you to donate money to sponsor an animal (or animals) such that his/her adoption fee and care costs are covered. That's pretty awesome. This means that if the organization is one of quality, it does all the work of making sure the placement of the pet is a good fit. Importantly, it also means that they are provided with money to sustain the care of the animal or animals until its "fur-ever" home is secured.

Naming Rights. You may have noticed that some zoo or aquarium exhibits have a person or family name attached to them. This is because the person or family contributed in an amount that is large enough to merit this action. We lived near a zoo for many years when my kiddos were small. The zoo carousel was sponsored by a particular family and for a time, the family donated funds so that all rides were no cost. I do not know about you but having a carousel at the zoo named after my family or my pet that also gave free rides to families would be kind of the best thing ever. Of course, these types of gifts usually require a substantial amount of money.

Community Foundations. You may be surprised to learn that many cities, even the moderately sized, have a community foundation which benefits the citizens of that city. In its most basic form, people contribute money into a fund or funds and the foundation distributes some of it every year to certain charitable organizations. Some foundations allow you to establish an endowed fund that is used for a specific type of organization. Under this arrangement, you might, for example, be able to designate charities which help animals. In my view, the most wonderful thing about it is that it's a continuous gift and the local foundations do all of the heavy lifting in terms of paperwork, etc.

Pet Burials

Human beings have been buried alongside their animals for millennia. Ancient Egyptian records show that pets from birds to cats to crocodiles were mummified and buried with humans as sacred offerings to Egypt's many gods. In fact, researchers believe more than 70 million animals were mummified between 800 B.C. and 400 A.D.

Cemeteries specifically for pets were first created in the 1890s, and some are still around today. As with the loss of any loved one, the burial of a pet is about comfort for those left behind and it also offers a place to visit.

These days there are even funerals for pets so that the surviving pet families can grieve. In fact, many options are available concerning pet death. Some places allow cremation, burial, caskets, monuments, funeral services, and even pre-planning.

Certain states have specific laws that address pet burials and cemeteries. New York has such a law and when I reviewed it, I noted how eloquent the wording is in stating its purpose. I was so taken by the rationale that New York has for allowing pet cemeteries to exist that I have placed an excerpt of the law below:

> "The legislature hereby finds and declares that the relationships that humans develop with other members of the animal kingdom that are taken into our homes and kept as pets are unique and special. These relationships can enrich our lives and increase our happiness. Even after the death of a pet, human attachment to the memory of the pet often remains very strong and many people feel the need to memorialize their love for their animal by burying their pet in a pet cemetery. Pet cemeteries, their managers and owners have a special responsibility to their customers who have entrusted their pets' re-

mains with them. These pet cemeteries have a duty to act in an ethical and lawful manner to prevent grieving pet owners from experiencing further any emotional pain or financial manipulation. Perpetrations of fraud against grieving pet owners are unconscionable. The legislature further finds and declares that the people of this State have a vital interest in the establishment, maintenance and preservation of pet cemeteries and pet crematoriums and the proper operation of the businesses and individuals which own and manage the same. This article is determined an exercise of the police powers of this State to protect the well-being of our citizens, to promote the public welfare, to promote the health of the public and to prevent pet cemeteries and pet crematoriums from falling into disrepair and dilapidation and becoming a burden upon the community."

Beautiful. It publicly acknowledges our need to bury and respect a pet family member.

Years ago my brother's dog, Frank, died, and Frank was placed at a pet cemetery in Ohio. We all loved Frank; my parents still visit his resting place and my children have been as well. The cemetery has many different types of pets buried there. There are many dogs and cats but also horses, hamsters, birds, and a variety of others evidencing our love for those pets that gave us joy. Pet family members visit and some even decorate for occasions.

Here's one that is my favorite:

Here's Frankie's grave:

Of course, pet burials are not free; cemeteries require maintenance and up-keep. If a burial for your pet is important to you, then you have some options, including:

Pre-Paying for a cemetery plot and headstone. Just like for humans, you can make a pre-death arrangement with a pet cemetery for the place of burial. As you can see from the above photos, headstones can be individualized for your pet.

Placing provisions in your Pet Trust. Setting funds aside for this in your estate planning documents for any pet that may outlive you needs to be addressed with your estate planning attorney; this can be done inside your Pet Trust. Here's an example of a provision that could be included in a Pet Trust:

> If my dog, CAMMIE dies prior to complete distribution of the principal of her trust, the Trustee may, in the Trustee's discretion, pay from her Trust the expenses of her last illness, the costs of burial at a pet cemetery, headstone, and related expenses. It is my preference that CAMMIE be placed at XXX Pet Cemetery with a small headstone.

Distribution to Pet Custodian. If pre-planning with burial arrangements or with a Pet Trust is not for you, your estate planning documents can provide that a certain amount can go to your Pet Custodian with directions for use. For example, you can give $7,500 to your Pet Custodian for the care of your pet with the direction that you would like any amount left at the death of a pet to go for burial. Of course, there will be no legal obligation on the part of your Pet Custodian to comply with your wishes; however, usually, a Pet Custodian is a friend or family member and fellow pet lover, so he or she will likely do as you instructed.

Pet Cemeteries

A pet cemetery can actually be an interesting travel destination. For those who love pets (and if you are reading this book...), there are some places that are worthwhile, relaxing, and thought- provoking. Here are a few that I have discovered:

Hartsdale Pet Cemetery. Located in New York, this cemetery claims to be the oldest in the world, having been established in 1896 by a New York Veterinarian. Today the cemetery is the final resting place for over 80,000 pets. Hartsdale is home to a variety of pets including exotic animals like monkeys and a lion cub. Gravestones of every kind offer expressions of love, humor, and devotion.

The National War Dog Cemetery. Dogs have served our country in the military for many years. In honor of that service, in 1994, the National War Dog Cemetery was officially dedicated at the U.S. Marine base in Guam. This came about because in 1944 during the Battle of Guam, a dog named Kurt warned soldiers about an oncoming attack. It is said that Kurt saved the lives of about 250 Marines. 250! Kurt was a true hero. Kurt died in the arms of 1st Lt William Putney, a veterinarian and the commanding officer of the 3rd War Dog Platoon.

Kurt and other dogs killed in action were buried in a portion of the temporary Marine cemetery. In the 1980s Dr. Putney returned to Guam to find that the cemetery for the war dogs had been largely forgotten. Thanks to his efforts, the National War Dog Cemetery was opened. What's very special about this is the "Always Faithful" monument that Dr. Putney and various organizations raised funds to install, to honor the dogs that lost their lives saving our soldiers and liberating Guam.

Kurt is memorialized in the Always Faithful Monument. In addition to Guam, this monument can be found at Auburn University College of Veterinary Medicine, Auburn, Alabama; the University of Tennessee's College of Veterinary Medicine in Knoxville; and The American Kennel Club Museum of the Dog.

CHAPTER 6

Estate Planning When You Have An Exotic Animal

N o matter who you are to me and how much I adore and love you, I am *never* taking your pet spider, lion, pig, monkey, kangaroo, lizard, or snake. Never. It's not going to happen. My guess is that your family and loved ones could have similar feelings.

Finding someone with the desire to take in your exotic animal isn't the only challenge; consider, many don't have the capability to house and physically take care of an exotic animal. There are many factors involved: enclosure; attention to the animal; the cost of feeding; the cost of medical care; and placement in an environment that promotes the best life for the exotic pet.

What this means is that those with exotic animals must take extra special care in their estate planning. This chapter is designed to help.

A Unique Skill

If you have an exotic animal, then I presume that you have the capacity to do what's necessary for the care and happiness of that animal. And, you must realize, that this is not a skill shared by many others. If the care of an exotic requires a Herculean effort and Hercules types are few and far between (they are), then an examination of your estate planning is more urgent. Here's an example:

Jim lives in a rural area and has dedicated his life to the care of injured owls who cannot be rehabilitated into the wild. At any given time, there are fifteen owls in his care. His daily obligations are to provide food, water, and to clean the enclosure. In addition to daily chores, he has to make sure that the owls are seen by a vet familiar with owls who will come to where they live to dispense the necessary immunizations and do check-ups and well visits. All of this is expensive and time-consuming. Jim is able to make this work because he is retired and has a pension that allows him to this provide this care.

Since Jim's care of these owls is a one-man effort supported solely by him, Jim needs to consider what will occur in the event of his incapacity or death. This includes pre-planning, the actual planning, and some degree of preparation.

Pre-Planning for Your Exotic Animal

Because there may not be a family member or friend willing to take in an exotic animal if something happens to its owner, it's important to think about how things will play out in that situation. It's not like there are many places that house orphaned exotics, as with shelters for dogs and cats. It is therefore important that you have a plan in place. Pre-planning means making decisions now; it is a must in this scenario. Here's what you need to do:

- Arrange *where* the exotic animal or animals will go
- Put into place the Exotic Pet Custodian who will be in charge of the exotic animal
- Arrange for *how* the exotic animal will get to the new location
- Plan for the funds to take care of your exotic animal in your absence

Arranging Where your Exotic Animal Will Go. Placing your exotic animal depends upon what type of animal you have. A lion, for example, is going to be harder to place than a snake. Nonetheless, any exotic animal owner needs to have a Plan A and a Plan B in place in the event of his or her incapacity or death. Basically, your options are to find a competent person or an organization that is willing and able take your exotic animal.

Choosing A Person. If you have a person in your life who can and will take your exotic animal, that is fantastic. Make sure he or she is willing to step into your shoes and consider whether he or she can expend the financial resources that your exotic requires. If the person you choose is long on care and ability but short on funds, it's important that your estate planning documents are drafted to provide him/her with financial support for the animal's care.

If no one will take your exotic animal, one option is to find and train someone who is willing to do the job. This will often require paying them and then setting them up with the appropriate resources.

Under all circumstances, any person who is considering taking your exotic needs to have a place for it that is compliant with the laws governing its care and control. See below: *Legal Stuff.*

Note that you could also have a Pet Custodian work in conjunction with the placement of your exotic animal (see below). You can, for example, have a wildlife entity that houses your animals and still have a Pet Custodian that reports back to a Pet Trustee. Your estate planning documents can mean giving legal rights to a specific person(s) with regard to your exotic animal. For example, your Exotic Pet Custodian can be charged with facilitating the travel of your pet to a new location. Funds could also be used by the Pet Custodian to check on your animal. If the animal isn't being cared for, then he or she could have the power to re-locate. The abilities of your Pet Custodian can and should be specific to your situation.

Placement with an Organization. Another option is to research places that take care of exotic animals like yours.

Many people assume that a local zoo would take your animal if it were unique enough; however, that is not necessarily so. Many times, zoos have very strict requirements about taking in animals. Factors that may be taken into consideration include whether the animal is on the endangered list; the animal's genetics, the cost of upkeep associated with the animal; and whether a living space is currently available on the zoo grounds.

Animal habitats not designated as zoos are another option that people consider for their exotics. Since I have human children, I think I pretty much have been to every single habitat within a 200-mile radius of my home. So many, in fact, that I may have developed a keen eye regarding certain criteria that, in my opinion, make an organization "reputable." Things like the size of an animal enclosure are particularly important to me. When an animal's living area is too small, it breaks my heart. I do not want to be trapped in a closet all day long and I assume that animals do not as well.

One issue you may want to address is if the organization has sufficient liability coverage in case your animal causes harm. You would want insurance in place to protect your Pet Trust from a lawsuit because if your Trust runs out of money, it could mean that your pet doesn't receive the care you envisioned. If the entity you choose does not have sufficient insurance coverage, your Pet Trustee may want to pay for this or you may want to choose another place for your animal.

I recommend researching the organizations that are your best match and then visiting them and speaking to those in charge about their willingness to care for your exotic in the event that you cannot. If possible, placing a written plan in place with them is the best course of action. An institution may be more willing to take your exotic if they know that you have made provisions in your estate planning document which will help with the cost of care.

Funds for Care

There are many ways to give money for the care of your exotic animal. Here are several of them:

Planning in your estate planning documents. You can direct in your estate planning documents that certain funds will go for the care of your exotic. Options include an outright gift to your Exotic Pet Custodian (with the understanding that the funds will go toward care of the pet although technically there would not be any legal protection if the Exotic Pet Custodian did not comply with your wishes); placing funds in a Pet Trust; or designating money to an organization that agrees to take your pet. In any event, these gifts do not come into existence until your death.

Insurance Planning. Some clients take out life insurance policies for the specific purpose of funding the care of an expensive animal upon their death. Doing so could make sense, for example, if you have many exotic animals and the upkeep is very costly. If you are healthy enough to qualify, then purchasing a life insurance policy on your life with the beneficiary designation to your Pet Trust or to an organization could mean sustaining the cost and care for your animals when you are gone.

In our example above, Jim took care of injured owls. Let's assume that Jim used insurance to fund care for his owls in his estate planning. This is how it might unfold:

> *Jim took out a term life insurance policy for $250,000 on his life. Because he is in good health his monthly premiums are within his budget. Jim locates a wild animal sanctuary four hours away that is willing to take all his owls if something should happen to him. He updates his estate planning documents to include a Pet Trust. He names that Pet Trust as the beneficiary of his newly purchased life insurance. He names his good friend as his Pet Custodian to facilitate the transfer of the owls to their new home. He names another good friend as the Trustee of his Pet Trust with instruction to pay for all of the costs of his owls each month until the last one dies or until the Pet Trust runs out of money. His Pet Custodian and Trustee are to look in on his owls periodically and can move them if they are not being properly cared for.*

Jim's plan works because he thought through what would happen at his death and allocated a source of funds to making his plan a reality.

Outright gift. A person can make a gift while they are alive to any person or organization; in this case, it would be earmarked for the care of your exotic pet. The risk in doing this is that there is no contractual obligation that would require care for your exotic and also that the organization can go out of business.

An agreement with an organization or entity. Many charities have written documents which summarize an agreement to give money to them. For example, you agree that the organization will receive $30,000 upon your death and the organization agrees to house your exotic animal. If you are going to contractually obligate yourself to make a gift in your estate planning or otherwise, it is appropriate for all of the terms to be spelled out.

Exotic Animal: Legal Stuff

It's possible that there are rules about the care of your exotic animal at the federal, state, and local levels. Take care to check on any regulations, and make sure your Exotic Pet Custodian or organization is aware that they too must know and comply with those rules. Here is an introduction to some of the directives.

Federal Law. An exotic animal may require a license by the U.S. Department of Agriculture (USDA). Beyond that, ownership of the animal may be regulated by federal law and subject to additional conditions. These conditions can be regarding enclosures, treatment, and care. Relevant laws include the ESA, the Captive Wildlife Safety Act (CWSA), and the Animal Welfare Act (AWA). Here are some interesting federal laws:

1) One regulation prohibits a person from possessing, selling, delivering, carrying, transporting, importing, exporting, or shipping, by any means whatsoever, any endangered species of fish or wildlife. For our purposes, if you have an exotic that is covered under this law, it means that the transport of your exotic animal to its new destination after your death must be planned out in advance.

2) Another law prohibits the interstate commerce of live big cats across state lines or U.S. borders unless the person qualifies for an exemption. Big cats covered by this law include lions, tigers, leopards, snow leopards, clouded leopards, jaguars, cheetahs, and cougars; all subspecies of these species; and hybrid combinations of these species. Penalties can result in jail terms of up to five years and fines of up to $500,000. So the takeaway is to not allow your Exotic Animal Custodian to cross state lines with your big cat without compliance with the law.

State Law. The definition of "exotic" pet can differ significantly from state to state. Some states have no laws at all while others have a complete ban on specific animals. Still others require a license or permit. In some jurisdictions with licensing requirements, individuals must obtain a permit, usually from the state fish and wildlife department, in order to own an exotic pet. Other states regulate (but do not ban or license) the possession of exotics, limiting the quantity of animals an individual may have, or setting standards for importation and animal care.

Local Laws. Your city or town may also have laws and regulations about exotic animals. There can be, for example, zoning ordinances which regulate animals living on your real estate. Sometimes health departments also have regulations. An internet search or a local zoo, humane society, or animal shelter are good resources for finding out information on this subject. If your city is large enough, some veterinarians may specialize in exotics.

Claims. There can be consequences for an exotic animal owner or seller/breeder if they violate a statute or if their animal causes injury to another. Claims against pet owners, breeders, and sellers will most likely be civil actions in which someone sues for money. Not only is being sued for money a possibility, an offending owner may be fined or imprisoned, and the animal may be taken, either to be euthanized or sent to a wildlife sanctuary. Additional information can be found at the U.S. Fish and Wildlife Service website (www.fws.gov).

Exotic Animal Issues: The Importance of Planning

For those with exotic animals, it's not enough to just hope that things will turn out okay. Arrangements need to be made in advance so that if the owner becomes unable to care for the animals, a plan for care and financial support is in place.

Above we used Jim as an example. Recall that he lives in a rural area and has dedicated his life to the care of injured owls who cannot be rehabilitated into the wild. Let's assume for a moment that Jim has a critical medical event that requires hospitalization for many weeks followed by home recovery, in bed, for at least another three months. If Jim has not planned ahead, then his owls are in trouble. In our example, the owls could not fend for themselves and therefore relied on Jim to sustain their lives. If Jim can speak and communicate, he might be able to give instruction and with help develop a plan for the owls, but he is officially in the management of a crisis.

Now imagine for a moment that Jim had died suddenly. Not only is there the immediate concern for the feeding and care of the owls; the issues become much more complicated. Someone will have to figure out things like whether the owls are Jim's property and must pass through probate; whether Jim's probate estate has the money to care for the animals while the person in charge determines where they go; and what happens in the event that a place for the owls can't be found and there is not enough money for their care.

Here are important steps to take in drawing up a plan for the care of your exotic animal:

- Research the best person or organization to take the exotic animal in the event of incapacity or death; confirm with the person or organization in advance with an agreement *and a plan* for care, drafted by a licensed attorney.
- Ensure that the person or entity receiving the exotic animal is in compliance with federal, state, and local law.
- Check to see whether the person or entity receiving the exotic animal has a proper habitat for it, including continued maintenance for the habitat.
- Find out whether there would be proper food and medical care for the animal.
- Check that the person or entity has sufficient property liability insurance to cover any event that could happen.
- Make sure there are funds available to carry out the care plan. If, for example, an exotic pet owner has an animal that is expensive to care for, then it would be important to allocate funds in a Trust or otherwise to cover those costs.
- Arrange for the transfer of the exotic animal to its new location, ensuring that the process is compliant with all laws which govern the transport of your particular pet.

CHAPTER 7

When Family Members Are Opposed To Pet Estate Planning

I once had a case where a man died and there were people living in his home after he died. These squatters refused to leave and I went to court and got the necessary papers such that they would be evicted. When my clients were permitted, they went into the home and found that the squatters left nothing in the home *except* the deceased man's dog. A real, live dog. The dog was left alone, in the summer, outside in the yard in the elements, unable to get out, and did not have food or water. Thank goodness, the dog was found in time, fed, and care and shelter were provided.

The above is an extreme example, but it exemplifies the point that for some people, animals/pets have no value. It follows that many people take the position that estate planning for pets is a joke or something not to be taken seriously. They may try to hinder or challenge your planning for your pets; this is especially so when a family member perceives that your pets are receiving money that should be coming to him or her.

What I want you to know is that your money is yours. Good planning means that you can leave it in the way that *you choose* that complies with the law of your state. These days, most states do allow for pet estate planning. That means that the law "has your back" on this subject. With the right estate plan, Pet Custodian, and attorney, troublesome family members will have a very hard time un-doing your wishes.

This chapter covers how to deal with family members who present a problem when it comes time to implement an estate plan that provides for a pet.

What To Tell Your Family About Your Estate Planning

People frequently ask me whether they should share the contents of their estate planning documents with their family members. My response is that it depends upon your situation, but in general I recommend:

Disclose the existence of estate planning documents to those with leadership roles. I most definitely suggest you tell your people who have a leadership role (such as Executor, Trustee, Pet Custodian, etc.) the following:

- that the estate planning documents have been completed
- that they have an important role should anything happen to you but that you could reevaluate as things change in the future
- that you would like them to commit to do the job (whatever it may be), but that they can decline (because you have an alternate)
- where the documents are located and that they do or do not have access

What you want your important people to know is that your estate planning is done and that if something happens to you, they have a role. This means that if, for example, you have a sudden medical event, that your important people will know that you have the right documents in place with a designation of who is in charge, and that they know where to look to find the documents.

Many times, providing access to people that have leadership roles may be the best way to handle things. I typically do not recommend giving out actual copies of your estate planning documents, for many reasons. First, you lose the ability to control who sees them and worse, documents such as your Power of Attorney (the financial document) could fall into the wrong hands and then used in a manner that harms you. Second, people lose things or they put them in a "safe" location and then forget what the location was. Your documents need to be in a place that is secure, such as a safe deposit box at a bank, that your important people can access.

Last, I find that sometimes telling some people what your documents say will result in those people having an opinion about what you should and should not do. Here's an example:

> *Claire completes her estate planning documents. She holds a "family meeting" explaining to her three adult children who are in charge under the terms of the documents and that she made certain gifts made to various charitable organizations that support the care of feral cats in her community upon her death. One child is particularly upset over this news and calls the lawyer who prepared the documents. When she does not get the response she wants from the lawyer, she hounds her mother constantly about changing the Will. She tells her mother that she wants to buy a home and that giving money to cats is stupid. Over time, her level of anger increases. She tells Claire that she will try to put her in a nursing home if the documents are not changed. Claire is miserable and wonders if she should just change it so that she can have some peace.*

As in the above example, providing open, unfettered access to your documents can result in hostility. This type of thing happens more than you might think, especially when family members feel entitled to assets. Yet how you leave your assets is not anyone's business except yours. Let's contrast this example with an alternate scenario:

> *Claire completed her estate planning documents. In them, she made several gifts to various charitable organizations that support the care of feral cats in her community. She places the documents in her safe deposit box at the bank. Claire's sister is the named Executrix, she knows that the documents are there, and she has access to Claire's safe deposit box where Claire's Will is kept. Claire dies and one of her daughters is very upset to learn of the charitable gifts. The daughter tells Claire's Executor that nothing should be given to anyone but her and her siblings. The Executor explains that Claire's Will was admitted to probate in her state and that the charities are legally entitled to the funds*

and will be receiving them. Claire's assets go in accordance with her wishes.

Choosing the Right Documents

If you have even a hint that your wishes will not be honored after you pass, then planning ahead can likely provide you with the security you need to feel confident that things will go as planned. In my view it comes down to these basic issues:

- Having the right documents
- Having the right language in the documents
- Naming the right people to be in charge

In earlier chapters we talked about the mechanics of a Last Will and Testament and a Pet Trust and what they do. However it's also important to know about document options that may be useful if family members attempt to cause trouble over estate planning for your pet. One such option is to have an estate planning instrument that is private and not subject to the public. With a private document, those who are not in leadership roles and who are not beneficiaries will not have access. A Revocable Trust is such an instrument.

The Revocable Trust

A revocable trust is also known as a "Revocable Living Trust," a "Living Trust," and/or a "Grantor Trust." The concepts surrounding a Revocable Trust are complicated and can be very hard for many (even lawyers) to grasp. The best way I have found to explain it is that a Revocable Trust is a fancier Last Will document – like a will but with more bells and whistles. It's designed for the most part to come into use after death. Like a Last Will, it can be changed or revoked during life.

How Revocable Living Trusts work in estate planning. Basically, a Revocable Trust creates a trust entity that allows you to transfer ownership of your assets into it while you are alive. Assets can be anything with title (title is how an asset is held for legal purposes) such as a home, car, boat, checking account etc. These assets are placed under the control of a "Trustee" who is in charge of the assets during your life and at your death. The Trustee during your life is most often the person who created the Trust. In other words, you are your own Trustee. At your death or incapacity, your spouse or another trusted loved one is typically the alternate who will take over as the next Trustee.

Common Questions About Revocable Trusts

If you have a Revocable Trust, do you still need a Last Will? Yes. In an estate plan with a Revocable Trust, there are at least two documents, a Last Will *and* a Revocable Trust. But wait! you might be asking, "If I have a Revocable Trust, why do I also need a Last Will?" The answer is that having a Revocable Trust does not necessarily mean that you will avoid probate and not need a Last Will. This is because not all assets will be subject to a Revocable Trust; they might go into probate instead – this depends upon the asset's title at your death. Stated simply, just because you have a Revocable Trust does not necessarily mean you will avoid probate. Let's review that again: *Just because you have a Revocable Trust does not necessarily mean you will avoid probate.* Again, how an asset will pass depends upon title. For example:

> **Assets with a Beneficiary Designation**. Assets like retirement accounts, annuities, and life insurance typically come with the ability to complete a beneficiary designation form to name a beneficiary or beneficiaries. If you pass away and the beneficiary is alive (if it is a person) or in existence (if it is a charity), they can get your assets by completing forms and submitting your death certificate. These assets do not pass through your Will or your Revocable Trust. You can, however, make them subject to your Will by naming your "estate" as the beneficiary. You can do the same with your Revocable Trust by naming your Revocable Trust as the beneficiary.

> **Assets in Your Own Name**. When you die and you have an asset like a bank account or car in your name alone, your loved ones cannot just re-title those assets as they see fit. No. Those assets come through your Last Will and Testament. If you do not have a Last Will, then the state

in which you live dictates the distribution of those assets. People with a Revocable Trust have a Last Will to capture any asset coming though the Will. These Wills say that when probate is over, the asset goes to the Revocable Trust for distribution.

Assets Titled in Your Revocable Trust. If you create a Revocable Trust during your lifetime and title assets in the name of your Revocable Trust, when you die, those assets will be distributed however your Revocable Trust says. The Revocable Trust document will not be made public and the assets inside skip probate.

When some people create a Revocable Trust, they believe that they are automatically avoiding probate with every asset, but whether or not this occurs depends upon how the asset is titled. (See above.) While it's complicated, a Revocable Trust can provide privacy from prying eyes.

Is it possible for me to avoid probate without a Revocable Trust? Yes, it's *possible* but it depends upon your state and how your assets are titled at the time of death.

What are some good reasons to have a Revocable Living Trust? For our purposes, there are two good reasons to have a Revocable Trust and both have to do with privacy.

Privacy as to who gets what and when. Most Wills are filed in the courthouse when you die which means that anyone can go and get a copy. However, a Revocable Trust is private and is not generally put on record for the whole world to see. Thus, any provisions for your pets inside a Revocable Trust would not be public.

Privacy as to assets in the Revocable Trust. Generally, if an asset goes to probate, the court needs to know the value of the asset. However, assets placed in a Revocable Trust *during your life* can skip probate since they are already in the trust. This means that the public does not get to see that asset.

As an example, assume you own a life insurance policy with a $200,000 death benefit. If your estate is the beneficiary, then chances are it would be accounted for in the public forum, meaning anyone could look at your probate and see that the asset exists. However, if you named your Revocable Trust as the beneficiary, then the check would have been payable to the Revocable Trust and it would *not* be subject to the public probate.

Fill-in-the blank Revocable Trust forms: possibility for harm. The complexity of doing a Revocable Trust is one of the reasons why some people use "fill-in-the-blank" forms. These forms typically come from companies that target the frugal with promises to save money and to achieve probate avoidance. This is frustrating to me, as it's so easy to employ scare tactics to try and convince people that they can miraculously save money with one of these vehicles. The truth is that when these documents actually come into play, there may be issues that cannot be resolved. In short, someone can sell it and then not be responsible for the document working the way it was promised to have worked, and the person who bought it isn't around to explain anything.

You have options when it comes to estate planning. If you are making arrangements for your fur babies and also if there is a family member who may cause trouble, it seems obvious that you would choose a real attorney – one who practices law in your state and in your town --who has the knowledge and ability to make recommendations and effectuate your wishes in a manner that is best for you.

Misconceptions about Revocable Living Trusts. These documents are often over-used and widely misunderstood. Some unscrupulous people would have you believe that a "living trust" has magic! It protects assets from the nursing home or allows tax avoidance. No.

I mean just think for a moment about this. Think of all of the nursing homes in every state and city in America. Do you actually believe that if a person just re-titles her assets and puts them in a Revocable Trust, that he or she can keep or give away those assets such that the government must now pay all of his/her costs of full-time care? No. The situation is more that people are scammed into buying certain trusts on the promise that it can magically protect assets from nursing homes and taxes, but when it comes down to the time for saving the money, the seller of these dreams is nowhere to be found. There are indeed some advantages to having a Revocable Trust and for our purposes in assisting with trouble-making family members, trusts can provide one important tangible benefit: privacy.

Adding Consequences. If there is a pesky family member that may make trouble when the time comes, then consider placing consequence language in your estate planning documents. Here are a few options:

<u>Exclusion for Contesting</u>. This is a provision in your document that says that if someone tries to contest the terms of your estate planning documents, then they are completely omitted. This, of course, assumes that the person has something to lose. Here's an example:

> *Kianna decides to complete her estate planning. She finds a qualified attorney and the attorney complies with her wishes that one-half of her assets will be placed in a Pet Trust for her three cats. Her only child, a daughter who is an accountant, will receive the other half. Kianna's Pet Custodian for her cats is her longtime neighbor and friend, Rachel. Kianna is aware that her daughter is going to be very upset that anything will be left for the use and benefit of her cats. She believes that her daughter might even hire an attorney to try to "break" her documents after she dies. To combat this possibility, Kianna and her attorney decide to add language to her estate planning document which would omit her daughter if she tried to contest Kianna's estate planning. In fact, if her daughter tried to contest, the share for her daughter would then go to the local animal shelter. This means that Kianna's daughter could get nothing and would be giving up her ability to receive half of Kianna's assets. This is a strong incentive for Kianna's daughter not to contest her mother's wishes.*

<u>Reduction of Amount for Contesting</u>. Total exclusion as described above is kind of a nuclear option that basically says any contesting means you get zero. A not-so-harsh option may be just to reduce an allocation to a fussing loved one. So, if a person is getting, for example, a specific bequest of $30,000, and he or she contests, that amount would be reduced to $15,000. Here's an example of what Kianna's estate planning documents could say:

In the event that my child or a person on her behalf challenges any part of my Last Will and Testament or Revocable Trust pertaining to my Pet Trust, my Pet Custodian, or my Pet Trust Trustee, then the share for my daughter under ITEX VII of this document shall be reduced from fifty percent (50%) to ten percent (10%). The forty percent reduction amount shall then be allocated to my Pet Trust to be held and administered as therein provided. Further, the ten percent (10%) to my daughter shall be first applied toward legal fees to defend my estate planning documents.

Write it Down: Avoiding Disputes

Many times family members tell me what they think the now deceased person *would have* wanted. In the same family, I sometimes have many people telling me much different versions of what they think the deceased person's wishes were. They cannot all be right. For example, in the same family, three different siblings tell me that their mom's last dying wish was to give the family farm to just him/her. Let's assume that in the moments before mom was going to forever leave this earth, her last worry was who would take the farm. Now let's assume that she verbally gave the farm to three different people on three different occasions right before her death. Then, these three different people want me (the probate lawyer handling mom's estate) to give the same piece of property to three different people, none of whom want to share the farm, and all of whom insist that they are fulfilling mom's last wishes. Even if I was so inclined, I cannot, of course, give property to people just because of a supposed verbal gift.

Thankfully, mom's assets in her name are controlled by her estate planning documents and if she had none, then the state in which she lives says who gets it. However, the point is that once a person dies, people claim to know what he or she wanted. Having it written down in a way that reduces any doubt about what is going where means avoiding disputes.

If you suspect there will be an issue with family and friends who will not respect your pet estate planning, then planning in advance is the key to protecting your wishes. Hiring an attorney who knows your state laws and drafts documents that meet your needs provides protection.

Part Three

Finalizing Your Estate Plan

CHAPTER 8

Not Just Anyone Will Do: Choosing The Right Estate Planning Attorney

T he public seems to have the general perception that *any* lawyer can draft estate planning documents. But *can* and *should* are two different things. So often I see documents created by an attorney that are so poorly drafted, that the Court (and I) need to fix them after the person dies. This can be expensive and slow, and it can also frustrate the estate plan, fundamentally altering the "who gets what and when" part. Getting the right attorney to help you with your estate planning is critically important. This chapter provides guidance on making that decision.

How to Choose and Hire an Estate Planning Lawyer

In my opinion, you should conduct some research before engaging an attorney; it's important to look for certain traits and qualifications. Any and all research is worth the effort. Here's what to keep in mind:

The attorney should have experience in estate planning. Would you go to an urgent-care clinic for brain surgery? Would you do your own root canal? Unless it was your only option and you were going to die, probably not. The same reasoning applies here.

In hiring an attorney, you are making them responsible for the disposition of your assets (including your fur babies) after you are no longer on this earth. He or she will be the architect of this plan. The content of your estate planning documents will dictate *who* gets what, *when* your beneficiaries receive your assets, *how* they receive it, and *who* is in charge. This is not a drive-thru type of a job.

Your estate planning attorney should be someone who understands the complex laws that surround Wills and Trusts in your state. He or she needs to be able to draft estate planning documents that:

- comply with the law;
- withstand a challenge from anyone who is so inclined; and
- fulfill your wishes.

Your estate planning attorney must have the ability and experience to do *all* of the above. The problem I sometimes see is that the average *non*-lawyer has no idea how to distinguish between an attorney who meets these qualifications and one who likely does not. It would be nice (for the public) if on the front door of your attorney's office there were a sign that stated things such as peer ratings, number of Bar complaints, years in practice, and a range of fees charged. But alas, you are on your own to figure it out. I am here to help, however, and below are some suggestions that may assist you.

Research your attorney. Hiring your estate planning attorney is a big deal. Before this happens, you have the opportunity to make an informed decision about your attorney based on research that you do. Here are some options:

ACTEC. www.actec.org This stands for the American College of Trust and Estate Counsel. In my view, this is the gold standard for qualified trusts and estates attorneys; it is an organization just for attorneys who practice trusts and estates law and meet certain requirements. An attorney is invited to be a "fellow" after meeting these high standards. The website allows you to search for fellows by state.

Martindale Hubbell. www.martindale.com This is a legal directory. In the old days, it came in large bound books; today, it is online. Lawyers pay to be in it, but there is a rating portion that is peer reviewed by lawyers in the same community as the lawyer being rated. In other words, lawyers rate one another, and you get to see the result. A lawyer cannot pay for a rating. Since lawyers can be a very tough crowd, especially toward one another, a high "AV" rating can be difficult to obtain and is a real badge of honor for many as it means that you have received the highest rating from other lawyers that know you and your work. Thus, there are useful reasons to use Martindale Hubbell; one is that you can view the practice areas of the attorney, and another is that you can see what his or her peers think about the attorney. Note that if an attorney is not in there, it does not necessarily mean that he or he is unqualified; it may just mean that he or she has decided not to participate. However, if an attorney is listed, it can be helpful.

Recommendations by other attorneys. If you have an attorney friend in your area that you have confidence in, consider asking him or her to recommend an estate planning attorney; you can also ask if he or she knows the attorney that you are thinking about hiring. I find the attorney world to be kind of close knit; we tend to know each other or perhaps know the reputations of other attorneys. Ask for candor. No one is perfect, but you do not want to hire someone who is not capable of completing the tasks at hand.

Bar Association in your state. Each state has a Bar Association. Attorneys must be licensed to practice law in a state before they can perform legal services, and the Bar Association is the governing body over the licensed attorneys. Attorneys are subject to ethics rules, and if we violate a rule, the Bar Association could take away our license. Scary stuff. Getting turned in to the Bar is a very big deal.

It is a good idea to determine whether an attorney has had issues with his or her state Bar. This information may be available online from the Bar Association in your state or you could try contacting them by phone or e-mail.

Look at the website. Review what the attorney's website says about him or her. Remember that this is basically promotional material so take it with a grain of salt. You are looking for a website that is professional and provides useful details about the attorney like education, experience, etc.

Interview the attorney. This can be by phone, in person, or even e-mail. If it occurs in person, ask in advance if there will be a fee.

I like it when clients ask me questions about myself. One, I like to talk about myself, and two, it shows me that they are giving serious thought to who they will hire for estate planning. After all, engaging an attorney means that he or she will craft documents that could designate everything from who is responsible for minor children to who gets your assets, when they get them, the care of your pets, and who is in charge of this process. Pretty serious stuff.

Here are some potentially useful topics to discuss when speaking with an attorney you are considering hiring:

1) Ask him or her if they have issues making provisions for pets in estate planning documents. Laughing or mocking responses should mean a hasty good-bye. This is your estate planning; find someone who makes you feel comfortable, respected, and taken care of.

2) Ask how long he or she has been practicing. I was once a new lawyer, and I am not trying to pick on them, but new lawyers are...new, so consider that. In my view, a new lawyer should have an experienced attorney (at least ten years in the practice area) who supervises his or her work. Also note that just because a lawyer is age thirty-five or above does not mean that they are experienced. Some people go to law school as a second career and are older when they start.

3) If you do not already know from the website, ask if he or she is licensed to practice in your state. Also, ask about his or her estate planning experience. Responses like, "I took an online course and this will be my first will" are not good.

4) Inquire about what organizations he or she belongs to, and for how long. Responses that include the Probate/Estate Planning Section of the state bar can be an indication that the attorney does indeed focus on this area.

5) Ask about malpractice insurance. Attorneys generally have insurance in case they make a mistake. We are not perfect people. If we do make mistakes, then the malpractice insurance comes into play. In my state, estate planning is one of the most frequent areas for which there is malpractice. My guess is that this is because many attorneys wrongly assume that estate planning is easy and that their

law degree alone qualifies them to perform estate planning. This is an incorrect assumption in my view.

6) Ask what the attorney's "process" is for estate planning. This question should result in an answer that tells you how many meetings you might have; how long it will take to draft the documents; how many meetings or reviews take place after the drafts are done; who keeps the documents, etc.

7) Ask the attorney if he or she drafts his or her own documents or if they buy them from a "service." In my view, attorneys with a certain level of experience draft their *own* documents. I do not buy forms. Ever.

8) Ask yourself how you feel about this attorney.

   - Are you confident that this lawyer will make you comfortable with asking any questions and with drafting a plan that may include pets?
   - Will he or she be available to you for questions after you complete the documents?
   - Do you have the feeling that you are being sold something you may not need?
   - Are the documents fill-in-the blank? That's not a good sign.

9) If it is important to you that this attorney be there after you pass away, then consider the circumstances of the attorney and ask if he or she intends to move or retire in the near future.

The attorney needs to practice near where you live. It is my opinion that the attorney should be close or relatively close to where you live and should inform you of any change in circumstances. You should be able to talk to that person if necessary, and he/she needs to be responsible for his or her work. Several years into my practice, I had a remarkable opportunity to move two hours away and head the Trusts and Estates Department for a law firm in another city. I moved, and yet I still have contact with many previous clients whom I have had over the years. I informed all of them of my family's move before we left; it was – and continues to be – important to me that they know where I am and have access to me.

Attorney Fees for Estate Planning

Attorney fees depend upon what you want your attorney to do. Drafting a complex Trust that should last forty years or more is pretty serious business. It's not going to be (nor should it be) free nor should it break the bank (so to speak). That said, you should meet with a qualified estate planning attorney of your choice, tell him or her the situation, discuss your wishes, and ask how he or she charges. Some attorneys (such as me) generally bill for estate planning by flat fee. This means that the client knows what the price is upfront, or an approximation. I often give an estimated fee that is a range. A range allows me to be fair to the client and to me. The process of estimating my time is different from client to client, but it is important to me that they know in advance what the cost will be.

For an attorney who charges an hourly rate, ask for a range and have him or her write it down. A range of $4,000–$6,000 does not, for example, mean a bill of $20,000 or $150.

Personally, I like to treat my clients the way I like to be treated. The plumber, for example, cannot just come to my home and do whatever he wants without telling me what he is doing or what he'll charge. I need to know up front. I assume that my clients like the same treatment from me. That is, they should know what to expect, what we are going to do, how long will it take, and what my fees will be.

What to Expect at a Lawyer's Office

In my practice, for the average person/family, clients call me or my assistant and we send them an Estate Planning Questionnaire; then they come in to meet with me. There is no charge for this meeting. We meet for about an hour and talk about their lives, estate planning, probate, and the people who would be good choices to be in charge in the event of incapacity or death. After the meeting, I write them a letter with a summary of what we talked about. If necessary, I make recommendations for documents, and I generally provide them with a flat fee quote for doing the work so that they know up front what they will pay. If they hire me, we may meet one or several more times to discuss their wishes for their family.

When there is pet planning, often we talk in depth about the different scenarios available. When we have settled on the details, I draft the documents and mail them to the client for review. If the documents meet with the client's approval, he or she comes into my office to sign in my presence and the presence of witnesses and a notary.

In the vast majority of cases, the client takes the original documents and I keep scanned copies. Here are the reasons that I do not keep original estate planning documents:

- I could die, become incapacitated, or retire.
- The client could move away.
- My firm could re-locate, close, or merge with another firm.
- My firm will not necessarily know if a client dies.
- Whether or not I get hired for a probate or for a Last Will and Testament I drafted is up to the Executor.

Red Flags: Attorneys

There are people in this world who hold themselves out to be respectable when in fact they may not be. You may even know them or see them around town. Sometimes they work in crumbling office spaces but they can also work in a fancy downtown building. We want to trust people, but not all people are trustworthy. That's just life.

Like any other profession, there are a handful of attorneys that are not reputable. There are some that steal, that are incompetent, and that skate by the rules in a way that allows them to continue to operate while being potentially dangerous to you. Most are not like this; I have found that the majority of attorneys are hard-working people trying to make a living and serve their clients and the profession.

For our purposes, it would be important to know that your attorney should have your best interest at heart. Yes, attorneys get paid for the work we do, but outside of that we should *not* have a financial interest in your business; we should not (in my opinion) sell you things that make us a commission if we are also preparing your legal work; and most importantly, only in very rare situations should we place ourselves in positions of power (Executor, Trustee, etc.) *within* your estate planning documents. Said differently, be leery of any attorney who suggests that he or she be your Executor or Trustee. Of course, if the attorney is related to you by blood, marriage, or adoption; is a dear friend; or is a colleague, there are exceptions. Here, I am referring to where the lawyer is a stranger to your family.

I have seen situations where an attorney drafts estate planning documents for a client and then after the client dies, the children come to see me because the attorney who drafted the documents will not return phone calls or give them any information. What I sometimes discover is that the attorney in question is a Trustee and did not include provisions for the family to be able to terminate him/her, and that since the client died, there have been huge fees paid out to the attorney and little paid to the children. Although the children in these situations are adults, they are not attorneys; they do not understand what happened. The attorney "in charge" will now take the position that he is complying with the wishes of the deceased family member who wanted him to "handle" everything in the way he sees fit. This situation makes me want to scream. Not only does it present ethical problems for the attorney, but it depletes the client's hard-earned assets, *and* now we are in a situation whereby more attorneys and more money needs to be involved to try to make it right.

In my experience, the attorney who drafted the documents and who is the Trustee does not want to: (1) admit any wrongdoing or (2) give up his or her lucrative Trusteeship. Further, if legal action is taken to remove the Trustee, the Trustee will likely get to hire the attorney of his or her choice to fight it *with the Trust funds footing the bill*. Seriously, this happens.

Another thing to be careful about is "free" seminars that try to sell you fill-in-the-blank documents or that tout things like "Avoid Probate!" Sometimes these are opportunists trying to scare you into buying something out of fear. Ironically, I find that people can pay as much or more for fill-in-the blank stuff than they would for estate planning unique to them and prepared by a qualified estate planning attorney. My guess is if the client understood what was happening, different choices would be made.

If you feel the need to name your attorney as your Trustee or to attend a "free" seminar with fill-in-the-blank documents, see below: *Protecting You From You.*

Non-Attorney Professionals Who Purport to Do Attorney Work

Non-attorneys are not permitted to give you legal advice and draft documents on your behalf. While your financial planner may think he or she is qualified to draft your Last Will and Testament or your neighbor who used to work at the county clerk's office thinks he or she can do it, *only* an attorney licensed in your state can and should advise you on estate planning. Not to sound too preachy, but law school followed by a very difficult Bar exam, followed by purchasing malpractice insurance, followed by adherence to rules of ethics, followed by continuing legal education, followed by experience in the field are the criteria necessary to provide advice on the law. Nonetheless, people without these qualifications do estate planning. Here is an example:

> *Allen is fifty-four and has two adult children. He lives a quiet life and does not like to spend money. He belongs to a golf group that meets once a month; one of the other members is an accountant. Allen confides in the accountant that he does not have a Will. The accountant offers to draft Allen's estate planning documents for free and says that he will put in a Trust that "works like magic" to avoid probate. Allen goes to the accountant's office the next week and signs documents. Allen dies two years later. The accountant is the Trustee of the Trust and holds all of the assets for the lifetime of Allen's two children. Each year the accountant gives Allen's children $9,500 without allowing questions or inquiry. There are no bank statements provided to the children. The accountant takes an annual Trustee fee of $5,000. He divides the Trust into three different Trusts and takes a fee for "tax preparation" for each Trust of $4,500. After five years, the Trusts are out of money. The accountant received $92,500 in fees ($25,000 in Trustee fees and $67,500 in "tax preparation" fees). Each of Allen's children received a total of $47,500.*

There are lessons to be learned from the above example. One is that in many ways, estate planning presents the chance for an opportunist to take advantage. The reason is that when it's time for your assets to be transferred, you are dead. It's easy for a person of poor character to insist that your wishes are being followed because you will not be there to say otherwise.

Another lesson is that quality work is not free. Allen may have really felt good about himself after signing the documents prepared by the accountant. He probably thought he took care of business. I wonder what the "Allens" of the world would say if the conversation with his accountant about estate planning was honest and went something like this:

> *Allen: I am really worried that I do not have a Will. I have heard that probate will take my money but I have no idea. My health has not been good. What if something happens to me? I really want to put something in place but I do not know where to start. You're an accountant; do you have any advice for someone like me?*

> *Accountant: Sure. Come to my office. I am not a lawyer, but I downloaded a form that if you sign will put me in charge of your life's savings when you die. Your kids will each get about half of what I get. I will do as little work as I can and I will tell your kids that this Trust represents your last wishes. I will lie to them and tell them we were best friends so that they will believe me. Your kids will never guess that you had no idea I would spend your hard-earned money on myself and that we only casually knew each other. I will probably buy myself a fancy new car so that more people think I am reputable and I can do this again and again.*

If only the unscrupulous would say the truth! But you and I both know that does not happen. Rather, you are on your own to determine the best course of action.

If you do name a professional as Trustee or Executor or if you have a fill-in-the blank document, make sure to include in your documents escape hatches so that your people can fire someone who has started acting in a way that is harmful. This can take the form of giving a person in your life who does not stand to benefit financially from you the ability to review accountings, speak with the family, and determine if the professional is on the up and up.

Online or "Do-it-yourself" Estate Planning Documents

If you want a do-it-yourself estate plan, that is certainly an option. It's your life and you may feel that it's the best route to take. Consider, however, what we've covered earlier in the book – for instance, the complexity and importance of the documents that dictate what will happens if you're incapacitated or pass away. I have seen some of these do-it-yourself documents, and I have not been impressed. I know I cannot end the online or "kit" Will industry and I am not trying to do so, but ask yourself if your wishes and intentions can be satisfied by those means. Mine cannot.

Protecting You from You

There are some things that I am very good at, but many things are outside of my area of expertise. I do not, for example, do my own dentistry or plumbing. My point is, we all need help and advice for certain matters and unless you are a trust and estates attorney, you may benefit from the experience of one who has seen a lot (me). But if you insist on another route, here are just a few tips for protecting your family:

- Know how your assets are titled because that impacts how they will be distributed at your death.
- Tell your family who should take your fur baby. Even if you do not give them legal rights in estate planning documents, your family could (in theory) abide by your wishes.
- Keep good records. For example, maintain an up to date financial sheet that lists all of your accounts (including bank accounts, retirement accounts, and insurance policies) and their amounts, as well as any debts.

The above steps don't take much time and they can help your family members immeasurably.

CHAPTER 9

Preparation And Organization

Like most things in life, being prepared means saving money and time. This is true for estate planning. Creating an estate plan means protecting your funds for your loved ones and saving them the effort of having to sort everything out on their own. An estate plan also makes you better able to articulate the plan that suits your needs and gives you peace of mind. This is especially true with regard to your fur babies.

Goals For Your Estate Planning

Ask yourself these questions:

1) What do I hope to accomplish with estate planning?
2) What am I most concerned about if I should pass away?
3) Are the titles to my assets the way I want them such that I know which assets are and are not passing under my Will? (Look to bank accounts, life insurance, retirement accounts, and vehicle titles to determine which assets will go automatically to others and which will go by the terms of your Will.)
4) How do I want to leave my assets? Will I leave things to my spouse, children, siblings, charities, and pets?
5) Do I want to appoint a Pet Custodian for my pets?
6) Do I want to provide access to funds for my Pet Custodian?

7) Who are the people who are able and willing to step in and help with issues of money and asset distribution if I have passed away?

8) 8Who are the people who would step in and help if I am alive but unable to make decisions for myself about health care and money?

Planning Tips for Getting Your Estate Planning Completed

Planning Tip: Have an idea as to what kind of plan you want.

If you have reviewed the chapters of this book, you should have an idea of what kind of plan you may want. For example, you may think that having a Last Will and Testament with a Pet Trust would be the best way to go. Further, you may want the Trust to contain certain restrictions regarding how everything is distributed.

Planning Tip: Ask your important people if they are willing to be "your people"

Just because you may have the perfect person in your life to be your Executor or Trustee (see Chapter 10 checklists for the qualities to look for) does not mean that person can or will do the job. For most of us, the person who will do it (someone we trust and who is available!) may not be perfectly matched to the task. But their most important qualification is that they say *yes* – so perfect or not, ask the person (or people) that you are choosing if they are willing to do the job.

For jobs like Executor, your important person may not need to know what your documents say; rather, they just need to know that if the time comes, they may be called on to act.

The start of the conversation could go something like this:

> *You: Rachel, I have been working on my estate planning. Right now, I am thinking that perhaps you would be a good person to be in charge of my estate if I should pass. What are your thoughts about that? Would you be willing to have a discussion with me about what this would mean?*

Rachel would likely have some questions about it but in general, unless your death is eminent (for example, a terminal illness), Rachel would need to know that 1) she does not have to accept the job – there are others you can ask; 2) that the documents may be changed; and 3) that your important documents are at a certain location.

If you are naming a person for a really big job like the Trustee of a Pet Trust, the conversation likely should be more detailed and should involve at least the following: Explain how the Trust works (restrictions, etc.); explain your important person's responsibilities; and perhaps provide access to the attorney who drafted the documents so that the documents can be explained.

For me, the hard conversation was asking my Pet Custodian if she will take my dog in the event there is a family disaster. I am lucky; my person not only agreed, I have confidence that my pet would be treated the way I would want if I could be there myself.

Not everyone will want to be your important person. If he or she doesn't want to do it, that's perfectly okay; it's information you should know in advance before making your documents final.

Planning Tip: Research and choose an estate planning attorney

Review Chapter 8 for suggestions about choosing the right estate planning attorney for you.

Planning Tip: Have your information organized

It is unrealistic to think that when we die, we will have all of our paperwork and information updated and in perfect order. Most people do not live in that world. What *is* realistic and what I recommend to clients is to update their financial statement – a list of all the items that fall under the umbrella of your financial life – once a year. Tax time works for me as I am already thinking about that kind of paperwork.

After you are gone, the people who are in charge have to figure out what you had and dispose of or transfer it. Consider this typical situation where an adult daughter comes to see me about a parent who has passed away. The daughter says to me, "I don't know if Dad had a Will and other than his home I don't know what assets he had." In this scenario, my job as the probate lawyer is much more hands on (and expensive) than if the daughter came in and said, "My dad died, here is his Last Will putting me in charge. Dad had a home, a checking account, and a retirement account. I have the deed and his last three months' bank statements."

After Your Estate Planning Is Completed

You did it. Yay you! You should feel a sense of relief and pride that you have taken care of important business. There are just a few more steps to consider.

Keep your completed documents and information in a safe place.

There is no one perfect place to keep your signed original documents but there are *a lot* of places that are not perfect. In my world, there are two places where original estate planning documents are safe and relatively easy to locate: a safe at home or a lock box at a bank.

A safe in your home is beneficial because it can keep the documents secure and there is 24-hour-a-day access. That can be especially important for any health care document that may be needed. For example, imagine that your spouse had a medical emergency in the middle of the night; if his health care document is at a bank or at your attorney's office, you wouldn't be able to get to it.

I like the lock box option because many people do not have a safe in their home and it is a realistic place for your loved ones to look. However, make sure that at least one copy of your health care document is at your home in case you need to access it during non-bank hours.

Tell your important people (Executor, Alternate Executor, Trustee, Pet Custodian) where to find your documents and information.

If you die or become incapacitated, then you will no longer be able to convey this information. I get calls frequently from non-clients who look me up and know I am an attorney that practices probate law. They ask me where to look for a deceased person's Will. Lockbox, safe, home office? Sometimes I learn later that the documents were found in a place like the garage. That's just frustrating for everyone.

Keep a digital asset inventory.

This is an issue more and more as our online lives grow. Many people pay bills online and no longer get paper statements. We have social media of every kind and sort. When someone dies and all of their assets need to be sorted out, doing it right and once is the way to go. Make it easy on the people you are leaving behind and give them access to your important information. Put that information in a safe place so that only the people you choose will have the ability to retrieve it.

What could be in your safe or lock box

Your estate planning documents
Life insurance policies
A list of your assets
Deeds
A list of your passwords (or instruction on how to access an online password-keeping service)

Have your estate planning documents drafted and then review them every three to five years.

Things change, important people die, pets come into your life, relationships end and start. Reviewing your estate planning document in the years that follow the initial completion will likely not be a complicated and expensive endeavor. The good part is, it allows you to make sure any restrictions that you placed in the documents still comply with your wishes and your situation. In addition, it allows you to evaluate whether your important people (Executor, Trustee, and alternates) are still the right people for the job.

CHAPTER 10

Checklists

We've covered all the ways to pick the right people for your estate plan in earlier chapters. Here are checklists with all that information plus additional questions, designed to help you work through the process:

HIRING AN ESTATE PLANNING ATTORNEY

- Research
  - Is the attorney licensed in your home state?
  - Does the attorney concentrate on estate planning?
  - Does the attorney have sufficient experience to do your estate planning?
- Questions for potential hire
  - Tell me your estate planning experience
  - What is your opinion about including pets in estate planning?
  - Do you have malpractice insurance?
  - What is the process you typically have for estate planning?
  - How will I be charged?
  - Will I be charged for asking you questions after the documents are signed?
  - Is there someone who would take over for you if you died or could not practice?

- – Do you have an estate planning questionnaire for me to complete?
  - – What is your work schedule? Do you work full or part-time? Are there others in your office who could assist if something happened to you?
- – What to Expect at the First Attorney Meeting
  - – Review of your assets
  - – Review of the situation
  - – Express your goals for estate planning
  - – Learn what the lawyer recommends and how the plan would be implemented
  - – Provide full legal names of your beneficiaries and the people you want to be your important people (Executor, Trustee, Pet Custodian, etc.)
- – After the First Meeting
  - – Sign an engagement letter which states how you will be charged
  - – Receive a letter from the attorney which summarizes the proposed plan, asks for more information, or schedules another meeting
- – Review draft documents
- – Confirm that your important people will act if the time comes
- – Sign documents
- – Keep original documents in safe location
- – Prepare an updated financial statement and digital inventory and keep in a safe and secure place

CHOOSING AN EXECUTOR

- – Gets along with the beneficiaries
- – Is a responsible adult
- – Is a trustworthy person
- – Does not have a great deal of debt and access to money will not be a problem
- – Has held a job (or is retired) and some life experience

- Has a reasonable knowledge of finances
- Does not have mental or drug issues that would interfere
- Is involved in your life

CHOOSING A PET CUSTODIAN

- Loves your fur baby
- Is a responsible adult
- Is a trustworthy person
- Has a home which can accommodate your pet
- Has a home where your pet can live happily (for example, does not have animals that would harm your pet)

CHOOSING A TRUSTEE

- Qualities of a good *family member trustee*:
    - Is willing to do the job
    - Is a responsible adult
    - Is a trustworthy person
    - Has some knowledge of tax reporting and investments
    - Has a reasonable knowledge of finances
    - Has held a job (or is retired) and some life experience
    - Does not have mental or drug issues that would interfere
    - Is involved in your life
    - Will be able to operate under the restrictions of a Trust

- Choosing *a bank or trust company trustee:*
    - How long have they been in business?
    - Do they have a minimum Trust asset amount?
    - What is their process for Trust work?
    - What is their annual fee?
    - How do they treat beneficiaries when there is a dispute?
    - What is the investment strategy for the Trust assets?

- Choosing *a non-bank or trust company professional trustee:*

- What if you leave your job? Retire?
- What if you move away from my state?
- How much will you charge? When will this be charged?
- Will the fees be stated in writing?
- Would you charge a fee AND hire a lawyer/accountant?
- Have you been a trustee before?
- Have you ever filed for bankruptcy or been sued?
- Do you have insurance that allows you to be a trustee?
- Why would you do a better job than a family member?
- How would it work – what is your process for complying with the Trust terms?

CHOOSING AN ATTORNEY-IN-FACT/AGENT UNDER YOUR POWER OF ATTORNEY DOCUMENT

- Is the person being considered *available* to help?
- Is he/she responsible with money?
- Can he/she dedicate the time necessary to make good decisions for you?
- Is he/she trustworthy?
- Is he/she willing to take on this responsibility if necessary?
- Is he/she financially sound?
- Would he/she respect your wishes concerning your pet?

GLOSSARY

There are probably definitions of these words written into the laws in the state where you live. The definitions below give an explanation of the word that comports with a general meaning.

Administrator: a male person appointed by the Court in a probate proceeding where there is not a Last Will and Testament

Administratrix: a female person appointed by the Court in a probate proceeding where there is not a Last Will and Testament

Attorney-in-fact or agent: in some states, this refers to the person who is appointed under a Power of Attorney document

Beneficiary: a person entitled to an asset either from a Last Will and Testament, a Trust, or a beneficiary designation

Digital assets: your online assets and passwords

Disinheritance: intentionally omitting a person from receiving assets under your estate planning documents

Estate planning: planning who is in charge and what happens to certain assets and with regard to health care issues in documents valid in your home state. Documents include a Last Will and Testament, Revocable Living Trust, Power of Attorney, and Health Care Document.

Executor: a male person appointed by the Court in a probate proceeding where there is a Last Will and Testament

Executrix: a female person appointed by the Court in a probate proceeding where there is a Last Will and Testament

Grantor: a person or entity that creates a Trust. Also known as a settlor.

Health Care Surrogate: some states refer to a health care surrogate as the person to make medical decisions on your behalf when you cannot act for yourself. This is not the same in every state.

Last Will and Testament: a legal document that if executed in accordance with your state laws can state who gets what assets, when they get it, how they get it, and who is in charge. This document often only controls certain assets depending upon the title of that asset.

Living Will: a document that may allow you to make certain medical decisions for yourself and possibly name someone to make decisions for you if you cannot make them for yourself. Some states call this document Health Care Directive or medical power of attorney.

Notary public: a person sanctioned (often by the state in which they live) to be an objective witness to the signing of documentation.

Personal property: this generally refers to your assets that can be physically moved around such as household goods, furnishings, jewelry, dishes, and so forth.

Personal representative: any person in charge of a probate estate. This can include a person appointed under a Last Will and Testament or a person appointed when there is not a Last Will and Testament.

Pet Custodian: a person you choose to have custody of your pet in the event that you can no longer have custody because of incapacity or death.

Power of Attorney: a document that allows you to appoint someone to act for you with regard to your financial life. Some states may have medical powers of attorney that allow you to designate a health care surrogate.

Probate: the legal means by which a person's Last Will and Testament is made of record and for which there exists state mechanisms for the transfer of a deceased person's assets and the payment of creditors

Settlor: a person or entity that creates a Trust. Also known as a grantor.

Title: how an asset is legally owned

Trust: a legal entity that can hold assets for the benefit of a beneficiary and has rules and restrictions as to the distribution of the Trust assets

Trustee: the person who is legally in charge of a Trust

ABOUT THE AUTHOR

Kelli Brown is a practicing attorney, speaker, and author. In 2017 she published her first book, *Estate Planning When You Have An Addicted Child*. She is a doughnut lover, pet enthusiast, and a frequent speaker on all aspects of estate planning and probate.

Kelli lives in Louisville with her husband, Walter Hawkins, two children, Henry and Maddie, and one little furball of dog joy, Holly.

TO LEARN MORE ABOUT KELLI, GO TO:

Estateplanningbooks.com

www.ingramcontent.com/pod-product-compliance
Lightning Source LLC
Chambersburg PA
CBHW031900200326
41597CB00012B/494